CRICUT

ALL YOU NEED TO KNOW ABOUT CRICUT: DESIGN SPACE, EXPLORE, MACHINE, AND PROJECT IDEAS. ENJOY YOUR FREE TIME WITH BEAUTIFUL CRAFTS!

Samuel Blade

© **Copyright 2021 - All rights reserved.**

This document is geared towards providing exact and reliable information in regard to the topic and issue covered.

- From a Declaration of Principles which was accepted and approved equally by a Committee of the American Bar Association and a Committee of Publishers and Associations.

In no way is it legal to reproduce, duplicate, or transmit any part of this document in either electronic means or in printed format. All rights reserved.

The information provided herein is stated to be truthful and consistent, in that any liability, in terms of inattention or otherwise, by any usage or abuse of any policies, processes, or directions contained within is the solitary and utter responsibility of the recipient reader. Under no circumstances will any legal responsibility or blame be held against the publisher for any reparation, damages, or monetary loss due to the information herein, either directly or indirectly.

Respective authors own all copyrights not held by the publisher.

The information herein is offered for informational purposes solely and is universal as so. The presentation of the information is without contract or any type of guarantee assurance.

The trademarks that are used are without any consent, and the publication of the trademark is without permission or backing by the trademark owner. All trademarks and brands within this book are for clarifying purposes only and are owned by the owners themselves, not affiliated with this document.

Table of Content

TABLE OF CONTENTS OF CRICUT FOR BEGINNERS

INTRODUCTION **18**

    WHAT IS CRICUT AND WHAT IS THE PURPOSE OF CRICUT MACHINE? 18

CHAPTER 1: WHAT FUN CRAFTS CAN I DO WITH A CRICUT MACHINE? **25**

    VINYL DECALS AND STICKERS..25

    FABRIC CUTS 25

    SEWING PATTERNS 25

    BALSA WOOD CUTS 26

    THICK LEATHER CUTS.. 26

    HOMEMADE CARDS... 26

    JIGSAW PUZZLES 27

    CHRISTMAS TREE ORNAMENTS 27

    QUILTS..27

    FELT DOLLS AND SOFT TOYS 27

    T-SHIRT TRANSFERS 28

    BABY CLOTHES 28

    DOLL CLOTHES 28

    FABRIC APPLIQUÉS 28

CALLIGRAPHY SIGNS...29

JEWELRY MAKING..29

WEDDING INVITATIONS AND SAVE THE DATES..............................29

WEDDING MENUS, PLACE CARDS, AND FAVOR TAGS................30

COLORING BOOK 30

COASTERS 30

FABRIC KEYRINGS 31

HEADBANDS AND HAIR DECORATIONS 31

CUT-OUT CHRISTMAS TREE 31

CAKE TOPPERS 32

FRIDGE MAGNETS 32

WINDOW DECALS..32

SCRAPBOOKING EMBELLISHMENTS 33

CRAFT FOAM CUTS 33

BOXES AND 3D SHAPES 33

STENCILS 33

TEMPORARY TATTOOS 34

WASHI TAPE 34

ADDRESSED ENVELOPES 34

GLASSWARE DECALS 35

DECORATIONS 35

CUSHION TRANSFERS 35

GIFT TAGS 36

CLUTCH BAGS AND PURSES..36

CHAPTER 2: LATEST CRICUT MACHINES AND HOW TO CHOOSE THE BEST MACHINE FOR YOU............ 37

THE CRICUT MAKER 38
CRICUT EXPLORE AIR 2 39
CRICUT EXPLORE AIR 39
CRICUT EXPLORE 1 40
WHICH MACHINE IS BETTER FOR YOU? 41

CHAPTER 3: TOOLS AND ACCESSORIES FOR CRICUT 42

NECESSITIES... 42
VINYL OR IRON-ON 46
ADDITIONAL TOOLS 50

CHAPTER 4: THE MATERIALS YOUR CRICUT MACHINE NEEDS 52

MAIN MATERIALS 52
OTHER MATERIALS 58

CHAPTER 5: HOW WILL YOU USE YOUR CRICUT MACHINE? THE SETTING OF CRICUT MACHINE.... 60

SETTING UP THE MACHINE 60
USING CRICUT SOFTWARE 61
IMPUTING CARTRIDGES AND KEYPAD.. 62
LOADING AND UNLOADING YOUR PAPER 65

Selecting Shapes, Letters, and Phrases 66

How to Remove Your Cut from the Cutting Mat 70

Techniques for Cricut Cartridges 70

CHAPTER 6: MAINTENANCE OF THE MACHINE 82

Cutting Blade 82

Subscribe to Cricut Access 83

De-tack Your Cutting Mat 84

Keep Your Cutting Mat Covers 84

Cutting Mat 85

How to Clean a Cricut Mat 86

Cleaning the Cricut Machine 86

CHAPTER 7: TIPS AND TRICKS ON HOW TO START AND HOW TO MAKE YOUR FIRST PROJECT 89

10 Top Tips and Tactics for Success 89

Cutting with Your Cricut 90

Print and Cut 91

Writing with Your Cricut 92

Scoring with Your Cricut 92

Embossing with Your Cricut 92

Badges for Your Cricut 92

CHAPTER 8: FAQ FOR CRICUT 94

What Is a Cricut? 94

WHERE CAN I DOWNLOAD THE SOFTWARE FOR THE EXPLORE MACHINES? 94
WHERE CAN I DOWNLOAD THE SOFTWARE IF I AM ON MOBILE? 94
WHAT ARE THE DIFFERENCES BETWEEN THE MACHINES? 95
DOES MY MACHINE COME WITH A CARRY BAG OF SORTS? 96
WRITING AND SCORING, CAN I DO IT? 96
IS THE DESIGN SPACE THE SAME FOR BOTH THE CRICUT MAKER AND THE EXPLORE? 96
DOES THE CRICUT MAKER HAVE FAST MODE? 96
WHAT IS THE THICKEST MY CUTTING MATERIALS CAN BE FOR THE CRICUT EXPLORE MACHINES? 96
WHAT IS THE THICKEST MY CUTTING MATERIALS CAN BE FOR THE CRICUT MAKER? 97
DO I NEED THE INTERNET? 97
CAN DESIGN SPACE WORK ON MORE THAN ONE DEVICE? 97
HOW LONG DO IMAGES I HAVE PURCHASED STAY IN MY POSSESSION? 97
WHY IS MY MATERIAL TEARING ALL THE TIME AND WHAT CAN I DO TO STOP IT? 98
ARE MY OLD BLADES COMPATIBLE WITH THE CRICUT MAKER? .. 98
HOW DO I CHANGE THE BLADES AND ACCESSORIES? 98
DO I NEED A PRINTER TO USE MY CRICUT? 99

CHAPTER 9: CRICUT DICTIONARY 101

BACKING 101

- Bleed 101
- Bonded Fabric 102
- Blade 102
- Blade Housing 102
- Blank 103
- Brayer 103
- Bright Pad 103
- Butcher Paper 103
- Carriage 104
- Cartridge 104
- Cricut Maker Adaptive Tool System 104
- Cut Lines 104
- Cutting Mat 105
- Cut Screen 105
- Drive Housing 105
- EasyPress 105
- EasyPress Mat 106
- Firmware 106
- Go Button 106
- JPG File 107
- Kiss Cut 107
- Libraries 107
- PNG File 107
- Ready to Make Projects 107

SCRAPER TOOL 108

SELF-HEALING MAT 108

SVG FILE 108

TRANSFER SHEET/PAPER 108

WEEDING/REVERSE WEEDING 108

WEEDING TOOL 109

CONCLUSION 110

TABLE OF CONTENTS OF CRICUT DESIGN SPACE

INTRODUCTION 114

WHAT MACHINE SHOULD I BUY? 116

CRICUT ACCESS 119

DESIGN SPACE 121

CHAPTER 1: INTRODUCTION TO CRICUT DESIGN SPACE 123

THE DESIGN SPACE APPLICATION 123

YOUR FIRST DESIGN 125

WORKING WITH CRICUT DESIGN SPACE LAYERS PANEL 129

CHAPTER 2: OPEN AN ACCOUNT 130

COMPATIBILITY 131

SYSTEM REQUIREMENT 132

ONLINE/OFFLINE 133

Subscription 134

CHAPTER 3: DOWNLOADING AND INSTALLING DESIGN SPACE 136

First Step 136
Second Step 137
Third Step 137
Launching the Platform Downloading and Installing, Cricut Access 138
Downloading Cricut Design Space 138
Installing Cricut Design Space 140

CHAPTER 4: CANVAS 143

Design Space Canvas (Design Panel, Header, Zoom) 143
Setting Up Your Cricut Machine on Canvas 146
Design Space Environment 147
How to Use Design Space Canvas? 148
Canvas Editing Area 148
Top Editing Subpanel 149
Canvas—Toggle Menu 150
Project Name (Untitled*) 151
My Projects 151
Save Button 151
Maker (Machine) 152
Make It Button 153

    Bottom Editing Subpanel 153

    Undo/Redo 154

    Linotype 154

CHAPTER 5: CANVAS TIPS AND TRICKS 157

    Basic Design Space Keyboard Shortcuts 159

CHAPTER 6: HOW TO USE DESIGN SPACE............ 160

    Guidelines on Editing Layers in Cricut Design Space...... 160

    Uploading the SVG 160

    Editing an SVG 165

    Editing the SVG Colors 166

    Taking a Layer Out 167

    Organizing and Bringing Layers into Line 167

    Flattening the Layers 168

    Welding the Layers 168

    Searching for Free Images in the Cricut Design Space ... 168

    The Weld Tool 170

    The Slice Tool 172

CHAPTER 7: KEY TO DESIGN SPACE 175

    Rudimentary Tools 175

    Cricut Design Space Canvas Area 175

    The Right Panel 177

    Group, Ungroup, Duplicate and Delete 178

BLANK CANVAS 179

LAYER VISIBILITY 179

SLICE, WELD, ATTACH, FLATTEN, AND CONTOUR 180

COLOR SYNC 182

LEFT PANEL 183

NEW 184

TEMPLATES 184

PROJECTS 185

IMAGES 185

TEXT 186

SHAPES 186

UPLOAD 187

ELEMENTARY FUNCTIONS 187

TOP PANEL 188

FIRST SUBPANEL 188

SECOND SUBPANEL 190

UNDO & REDO 190

CHAPTER 8: HOW TO CREATE DIFFERENT OBJECTS 191

INSERTING IMAGES FROM CRICUT IMAGE LIBRARY 191

INSERTING AN IMAGE 192

SEARCHING FOR IMAGES 193

BROWSING IMAGES BY CATEGORY 193

HOW TO BROWSE AND SEARCH FOR CARTRIDGES 194

INSERTING BASIC SHAPES 196

WORKING WITH IMAGES 200

SELECTING MULTIPLE IMAGES 200

CHAPTER 9: TIPS AND TRICKS FOR DESIGN SPACE 202

SEARCH BY SYNONYM.. 202

GET MORE IMAGES FROM THE IMAGE SET 203

GET FREE IMAGES AND TEXT 204

ENJOY FREE FONTS 205

REMOVE GRIDLINES 206

CHANGE ANY LINE TO CUT, SCORE OR DRAW........................... 208

PLAY WITH PATTERNS 208

MOVE THINGS ON YOUR MAT... 211

CONNECT SEVERAL MACHINES SIMULTANEOUSLY.................... 211

CHANGE CUT SETTINGS FOR YOUR MATERIALS 212

ADJUST CUT PRESSURE.. 213

CHANGE THE SIZE OF YOUR MAT.. 214

CONCLUSION...216

TABLE OF CONTENTS OF CRICUT PROJECTS

INTRODUCTION 220

CHAPTER 1: CRICUT PROJECTS YOU CAN MAKE . 226

500 Cricut Ideas to Spark Your Imagination 226

CHAPTER 2: SOME PROJECT IDEAS TO TRY AND GET PRACTICE 248

Design Your T-shirt 248
Recipes Stickers 253
Floral Gold Flowerpot 256
Wedding Invitation 258
Designing a Card 260
Custom Notebooks 264
Decorate You Mug 266
Paper Flowers 270
Make Your Own Doormat 273
Leaf Banner 276
Make a 3D Paper Flower 278
Paper Luminary 281
Adorn Your Pillow or Cushion 283

CHAPTER 3: TIPS AND TRICKS FOR PROJECT IDEAS 285

Wood 285
Iron-on 286
Vinyl 289

CHAPTER 4: OTHER PROJECTS 291

Leafy Garland 291

Box 294

Shamrock Earrings 297

Handmade Flower Corsage 300

Felt Side Banner 304

Personalized Phone Cover 306

Paper Succulents in a Container 309

Creative Herbarium 312

Geometric Lampshade 316

Takeout-Style Boxes 317

Cricut Foil Streamers 319

CHAPTER 5: HOW TO MAKE YOUR FIRST ART SALE ONLINE 321

Setting up a Website 321

Advertising 323

Taking Orders and Shipping 324

Saving Money Using Your Cricut Machine for Business 324

CHAPTER 6: TROUBLESHOOTING 326

Optimizing Speed and Connection 326

Calibration of "Print then Cut" Is Not Working Properly 331

The Incorrect Cartridge Name Appears on the Cricut Screen 333

When Images Are Added to the Queue, the Cricut Machine Freezes 334
The Cricut Machine Keypad Has Glitches 335
Unloading or Loading the Mat Makes the Cricut Machine Freeze 337
During Cutting, the Carriage Does Not Travel Along the Track 338
When Loaded into the Cricut Machine, the Mat Becomes Crooked 339
During Cutting, the Machine Freezes 340
Red Banner Error Messages in Design Space 340

CONCLUSION 343

CRICUT FOR BEGINNERS

MASTER THE USE OF YOUR CRICUT MACHINE TO MAKE AMAZING AND BEAUTIFUL CRAFTS AND PROJECTS

Samuel Blade

Introduction

What Is Cricut and What Is the Purpose of Cricut Machine?

A Cricut machine is a cutting machine. It has the unique functionality of being able to cut different materials that you will need for your crafts and DIY projects. Some of these materials include paper, vinyl, and materials as thick as wood. Although they are hardware, Cricut machines are dependent on their connection with your devices like mobile phones and computers.

Cricut machines are a very fun tool to use because they allow you to create art from materials you may not have known existed, and they allow your creativity to take flight because with the use of Cricut machines, you are able to create new materials to aid your work, and these materials you create may not be found otherwise.

In a nutshell, you create designs and templates using the device to which your machine is connected (the phone or computer system). These designs are preloaded into the device to which your Cricut is connected, and you can make a lot of changes or modifications with these designs. These designs are what you preload into the Cricut and use them to cut/print the material you are looking to print, just the way you want it to be.

When it comes to how a Cricut works, there is a lot to be learned about it, but having access to your own Cricut machine is like opening yourself up to a whole new world. There is literally no limit to the number of awesome crafts you can make with the use of the Cricut machine.

The Cricut machine has numerous uses besides being a shaper of structures for a scrapbook. The models themselves can be utilized to make different things, for example, welcoming cards, divider enhancements, and so much more. You have to think innovatively. There are no restrictions, and if there are, they are only an illusion of your creative mind.

Electronic cutting machines are strong instruments for specialists, educators, creators who sell their work on Etsy, or any individual who needs to remove the unpredictable shape. You can utilize these machines to make ventures, for example, stickers, vinyl decals, custom cards, and gathering designs. They cut plans out of an assortment of materials, utilizing programming that allows you to transfer, make, or buy drawings to be cut. Also, frequently, in the event that you put in a pen rather than a cutting edge, they can draw as well. A snappy voyage through Instagram hashtags demonstrates the full scope of activities individuals make with these machines.

Remember that these machines have an expectation to learn and adapt, particularly with the product. Many people have heard of a Cricut machine and it's been making a big splash in the crafting world because of everything that you can do with it. You might be surprised that you would be able to work with this machine with a lot of different materials and it can be a really fun way to make some great items.

When Cricut machines first came out, you needed cartridges to be able to cut out your letters and the shapes that you want to use for your items but now, you don't need cartridges at all! Now everything is done digitally because everyone understands that we have great technology at our feet, and we should use it to our advantage.

Most Cricut machines will now work over Bluetooth or Wi-Fi as well, which means that you can use your iPad or if you have an iPhone, you can use this as well. You can also use this from your computer. This makes designing your passions easier than ever and you have a complete versatility that will help you be able to do what you want and have creative options for you.

All machines come with the following items:

- Practice project materials
- A power adapter
- A cutting machine
- Access to free projects that are ready to make
- A cutting mat that is twelve inches by twelve inches
- A USB cable
- A free membership (it's only a trial one) to access to Cricut
- Guide for making setup easy
- Fine point blade (that is premium) and housing for the blade

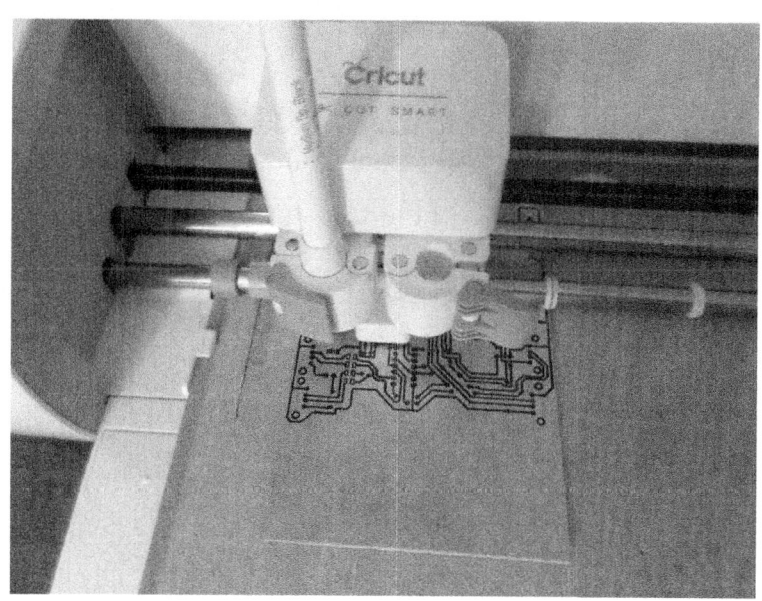

Another thing that you should know is that certain models come with additional items such as a specialized writing pen, different blades or even wheels.

A Cricut machine is a cutting machine. Specifically, it is known as a die-cutting machine. You can use it for paper crafting along with other crafting supplies as well. It's a machine that boasts of being excellent at crafting with precision. Many people think that these machines just cut paper, but they cut so much more than that.

Every machine will have its own software that is with its brand. It will be free to use and to download into or onto your machine. Cricut even has an app you can use. The app is friendly to the user and you are able to upload images and create designs. You can make your designs from scratch or purchase the designs from others. You can also upload images and purchase designs from the application and modify them to your custom designs.

The app is extremely easy to use and the software is very simple while being user-friendly as well. It gives you the freedom to have creativity with your projects. What you make in this will tell your machine where it needs to score or write. It also tells us where to cut.

If there is just one step, the machine can do a full design. However, if there are multiple steps, then your machine will convey this to you through the device that you have connected to it. It will tell you if you have additional steps as well.

A machine like this isn't necessarily a printer, though it can be said that it comes close. If you use the Print then Cut method it will let you have any design for your project, and it will take it from there for you to be able to use it properly. If you want to think about this easily, it would be a little like making stickers.

It also cuts more than paper. These machines are not just for die-hard scrapbookers anymore. It cuts so much more than that. As such, this book will include a master list of everything that will work with your machine and how to gain the most benefit from it.

Close your machine when you're not utilizing it to dodge residue subsiding into the cutting region. Wipe any residue or paper garbage away from the sharp edge and cutting zone with a perfect, dry material, yet simply after you've unplugged the machine.

The cutting mats for the majority of the machines accompany a plastic film to cover the glue side. Clutch these to expand the life of your cutting mats. You can likewise draw out your tangle's life by scratching ceaselessly any bits of material left on it after an undertaking utilizing a spatula device. When the adhesiveness has gone, you'll need to supplant the mats. You can discover stunts to invigorate the floor coverings, yet we've never attempted them.

Chapter 1: What Fun Crafts Can I Do with a Cricut Machine?

Vinyl Decals and Stickers

One of the projects you can carry out with the Cricut Maker is cutting vinyl and stickers.

You just have to create your design in Cricut Design Space, instruct the Maker to cut, then weed and transfer the design to whatever surface you choose.

Fabric Cuts

The presence of the Rotary Blade in the Cricut Maker makes it a well-respected machine. The Maker can cut any type of fabric, including chiffon, denim, silk and even heavy canvas. With this machine, you can definitely cut huge amounts of fabrics without using any backup, and this is because it comes equipped with a fabric cutting mat. Awesome machine!

Sewing Patterns

One major benefit of owning the Cricut Maker machine is the extensive library of sewing patterns that you'll have access to.

The library has hundreds of patterns, including some from Riley Blake Designs and Simplicity; all you need to do is select the pattern you want and the machine will do the cutting.

Balsa Wood Cuts

The knife blade, coupled with the 4 kg force of the machine, means that the Cricut Maker can easily cut through thick materials (up to 2.4 mm thick). With these features, thick materials that were off-limits for earlier Cricut machines are now being done.

Thick Leather Cuts

Just like balsa wood, the Cricut Maker is also used for thick leather cuts.

Homemade Cards

Paper crafters use the Cricut Maker because the power and precision of the machine make the cutting of cards and paper far quicker and easier. With the machine, homemade cards just got better.

Jigsaw Puzzles

With the Cricut Maker, crafters can make jigsaw puzzles because the knife blade cuts through much thicker materials than ever before.

Christmas Tree Ornaments

Cricut machine owners can easily make Christmas tree ornaments. All you have to do is go through the sewing library for Christmas patterns, use any fabric of your choice to cut out the pattern, and sew them together. Remember, the rotary blade cuts through all sorts of fabric.

Quilts

Thanks to the partnership between Cricut and Riley Blake Designs, Cricut Design Space now has a number of quilting patterns in the sewing pattern gallery.

The Cricut Maker is now used to cut quilting pieces with high precision before they are sewn together.

Felt Dolls and Soft Toys

The "felt dolls and clothes" pattern is one of the simplest designs in the sewing pattern library. Thus, it is used for homemade dolls and toys.

The process is easy; just select the pattern you want, cut, and then sew.

T-shirt Transfers

The Cricut Maker is used for cutting out heat transfer vinyl for crafters to transfer their designs to fabric. To achieve this, you have to make your design in Design Space, load the machine with your heat transfer vinyl, cut the material, and then iron the transfer onto the T-shirt. Alternatively, you can use the Cricut EasyPress to transfer the vinyl.

Baby Clothes

The Cricut Maker cannot cut adult clothing patterns because the mat size is only 12" x 24". However, you can easily make baby clothing patterns with the machine.

Doll Clothes

Just like baby clothes, the Cricut Maker can easily make doll clothing patterns because the mat size is big enough.

Fabric Appliqués

The bonded fabric blade doesn't come with the Cricut Maker, but if you buy it, you will be able to use your machine to cut complex fabric designs like appliqué. For the bonded fabric blade to cut effectively, there has to be bonded backing on the material.

Calligraphy Signs

The stand-out feature of the Cricut Maker is the Adaptive Tool System. With this feature, the machine will remain relevant in the foreseeable future because it fits with all the blades and tools of the explore series, as well as all future blades and tools made by Cricut.

The calligraphy pen is one of such tools, and it is ideal for sign and card making.

Jewelry Making

For crafters that like to explore jewelry making, the power of the Cricut Maker means that you can cut thicker materials, and while you can't cut things like diamonds, silver, or gold, you can definitely try to make a beautiful pair of leather earrings.

Wedding Invitations and Save the Dates

Weddings are capital intensive, and we all know how the so-called 'little' expenses, like save the dates and invitations, can add up to the huge cost. However, if you have the Cricut Maker machine, then you can make your invitations and save the dates yourself.

The Maker is capable of making invitations of the highest quality. It cuts out intricate paper designs and the calligraphy pen is very useful too.

Wedding Menus, Place Cards, and Favor Tags

The Cricut Maker is not restricted to the production of pre-wedding invitations and save the dates. With the machine, you can also produce other items such as place cards, wedding menus, favor tags, etc.

In order to keep the theme front and center, the crafter is advised to use a similar design for all their stationery.

Coloring Book

With the Cricut Maker, you can make 'mindful coloring' books from scratch. To achieve this goal, you need a beautiful design, a card, and paper. Then you command the Cricut Maker to create your personal and completely unique coloring book with the aid of the fine-point pen tool.

Coasters

In the sewing library, there are a number of beautiful coaster patterns and as such, the Maker is used to coasters.

With the Cricut Machine, you can work with materials such as metallic sheets, quilt, leather, and everything in between.

Fabric Keyrings

The Cricut Maker makes fabric keyrings and the process is simple—it cuts out the pattern and then sews it together. Besides, there are a number of designs for fabric keyrings in the sewing pattern library.

Headbands and Hair Decorations

The Cricut Maker is known to cut through materials like thick leather and this has gone on to inspire the production of intricate headbands and hair decorations. The machine is so inspiring; crafters in the fashion world use it for creative designs and projects.

Cut-Out Christmas Tree

It is a normal tradition for people to buy Christmas trees during the holiday season. However, if you don't have enough space for a big tree in your living room, or maybe you're allergic to pine, then you can definitely create your own Christmas tree.

The production of an interlocking wooden tree is something the Cricut Maker does easily because the blade is capable of cutting through thick materials like wood. With the Cricut Maker, you don't use a laser.

Cake Toppers

When Cricut bought over the cake cutter machine, the idea was to create shapes made of gum paste, fondant, and others.

It is obvious that the Cricut Maker can't cut as good as the cake machine; however, it can be used to produce tiny and intricate paper designs that can be used to decorate cakes.

Fridge Magnets

Cricut machines like the Maker and Explore Air are capable of cutting out magnetic materials. Thus, crafters can use the Maker to make those fancy magnetic designs placed on refrigerators.

Window Decals

If you're one of those who love to display inspiring quotes on your windows or even fancy little patterns on your car, then the Maker got you covered.

You just have to load the Maker with window cling and get your design created.

Scrapbooking Embellishments

The Cricut Maker is used for embellishments when scrapbooking. It is public knowledge that Cricut machines are super when it comes to cutting intricate designs. However, the Cricut Maker takes it to a whole new level, and the responsive new blades take away all forms of complexity.

Craft Foam Cuts

In the past, Cricut machines found it difficult to cut craft foam (especially the Explore machines); however, the Cricut Maker, with the 4 kg of force, cuts through craft foam very easily.

Boxes and 3D Shapes

The Cricut machines come with a scoring stylus and this tool can create items with the sharpest edges imaginable.

We all know that the Cricut Maker can execute all kinds of sewing patterns thrown at it. It can also cut paper crafts, including 3D shapes and boxes.

Stencils

The Maker comes in handy for people that create things that are used to create other items. The machine is incredible for making stencils, bearing in mind that you can utilize thicker materials to create the stencils.

Temporary Tattoos

If you're one of those people that want to have tattoos, but don't want them permanent for life, then the Cricut Maker is your go-to machine.

With the Cricut Maker, you can etch your design on a tattoo paper (mostly coated with transfer film) and use it on your skin.

Washi Tape

Crafters that use Washi tape for scrapbooking can testify how expensive it can be, especially when buying bulk from craft stores. However, those who own the Cricut machine can use it to cut out Washi sheets—they can print-and-cut their personal designs on it.

Addressed Envelopes

The Cricut Maker is an astounding machine that can save you from spending on certain items. Remember, we talked about making handmade wedding invitations; with the Cricut Machine, you can also make envelopes to go with the cards. Another good feature about the machine is that it is equipped with a calligraphy pen and a fine-point pen, meaning that it is capable of addressing your envelopes automatically. All you need to do is make sure that the words are clear enough for the postman to read.

Glassware Decals

With a Cricut Maker, you can cut vinyl to make glassware designs. People who host themed parties will love this one, e.g., if you're hosting a summer house party and you're serving mojitos, you can decorate your drinking glasses with coconuts and palm tree decals. Also, people holding Xmas parties can design and cut themed stickers to use on their cups.

Decorations

There are a couple of other desktop craft machines that are used to create general household decorations, but the Cricut Maker is one of the best—if not the very best.

With the Cricut Maker, you'll be empowered to create 3D wall hangings, beautiful cut-outs in the living room, and even things like signage in your closets, etc.

Cushion Transfers

With your Cricut Maker, you can brighten up your cushion and pillows by adding your homemade designs. With the flocked iron-on vinyl, you can create a lovely textured cushion using heat transfer vinyl on the Cricut machine.

Gift Tags

We all know that gift tags consume some of our money during the holiday season. However, with your Cricut Maker, you don't have to buy them anymore; you can just make your own.

Clutch Bags and Purses

The sewing pattern library is awesome; thus you can make different types of full-size purses, coin purses and even clutch bags.

Chapter 2: Latest Cricut Machines and How to Choose the Best Machine for You

This is definitely the most important thing that comes to your mind while you learn everything about the Cricut Machine.

Buying the best Cricut machine would complement your creativity and would help you create crafts, designs, projects, and ornaments. First of all, what you need to know about buying Cricut machines is that all Cricut machines work in the same way.

The thing that sets them apart or creates a difference in the Cricut machine is the unique features that are designated to them.

The similarity that every Cricut machine has is that each machine uses a free software called Design Space. It is important to know that every cutting machine has its own software, which is difficult to learn.

The most interesting thing about Cricut is that it is easier and more straightforward to use and create interesting things. You can download Design Craft and start using it even before you buy a Cricut machine. This would give you a good handle on Design Space, and you would be able to make things easier. If we are going to classify Cricut machines based on their features, then it would be as follows:

The Cricut Maker

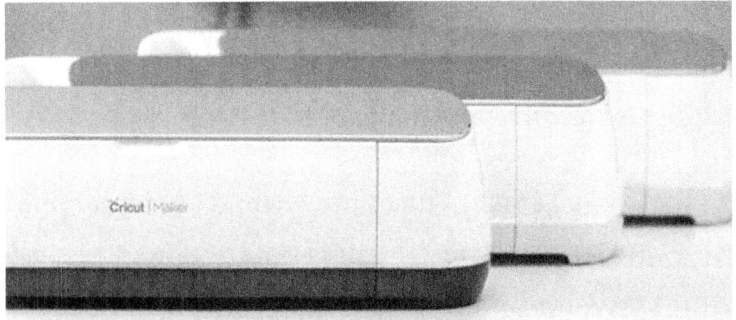

It is the most recent type of cutting machine that has yet to be released. Its specialty lies in its ability to cut wood and fabrics. The Cricut Maker is the only machine that has a rotary cutter for fabrics and crepe paper. To cut thick materials like wood, foam board, etc., Cricut Maker has now a knife blade installed in it that makes the wood cutting easier and better. The rotary cutter comes along with the packing of the Cricut Maker. But you will have to buy the knife blade separately. If you wish to change or switch different cutting tools, then you have to undo the clamp on side "B." After you have opened the clamp, put the tool of your choice and then close it. All this tells about how Cricut Maker is recently the best and extremely convenient to use.

Cricut Explore Air 2

Cricut Explore Air 2 is a diminution to the Cricut Maker. Although it is not compatible with the knife blade or rotary cutter, it can still cut hundreds of materials. It is better in a way that it cuts things twice faster than a Cricut Explore Air does. It is also cheaper than the Cricut Maker, usually less than half of the price.

Cricut Explore Air

It functions almost similar to Cricut Explore Air 2. The only difference is that this machine cuts a bit slower. As compared to Cricut Explore Air 2, the project thus takes time to finish.

Their prices are also almost the same.

That is why I would suggest you choose Cricut Explore Air 2 if you are facing difficulty in affording the Cricut Maker. It also has a Bluetooth embedded for wireless connections, making it convenient for Apple and Android users to feel the need to use the computer while using this machine.

Cricut Explore 1

Cricut Explore 1 is again a diminution to Cricut Explore Air. It is the first-ever Cricut machine that eliminated the need to use cartridges and introduced the internet Design Space feature allowing you to make designs and projects of your choice. The drawback that it has is that it does not have Bluetooth, so you need to attach a computer directly to it.

Otherwise, it would not work.

Which Machine Is Better for You?

With that being said, if you are looking for a Cricut machine at a reasonable price, then I would recommend you to buy Cricut Explore Air 2. It would also be easy to use if you are a beginner. But if you have enough budget, then Cricut Maker would definitely be the best option.

Chapter 3: Tools and Accessories for Cricut

You can't possibly use a Cricut machine alone, but the type of accessories or tools that you need depends on the kind of project that you're using the machine for. If you're going into home décor, you'll need different tools from those going into paper crafts.

Necessities

Irrespective of any project, some necessary accessories are essential. Some of these accessories come with Cricut, while some can be purchased from Cricut.

- **Cutting Mats**

Cutting mats come in three kinds, which are strong grip, standard grip, and light grip. You can also purchase any one of the sizes that they come in, which is either the 12 inches by 24 inches or the 12 inches by 12 inches mat.

The strong grip mat is ideal when you're cutting stiffened fabric, glitter cardstock, chipboard, specialty cardstock, and other thick materials. For thinner materials like embossed cardstock or standard cardstock, vinyl, pattern paper, or iron-on, we recommend the standard grip mat. For the lightest materials, a light grip mat is needed. Light materials include light cardstock, office paper, vellum, or other materials.

A newly bought Cricut machine includes a cutting mat in the box, and so you don't have to buy a mat separately. After a while, the mat will lose its stickiness and you can either apply glue to maintain it or buy a new one.

Also, when considering your project, you should get the right mat. If your mat is light grip and you try to cut a thick fabric, you might end up messing the entire project up because the material will keep on shifting from the mat.

- **Cutting Blades**

Cutting Blades are the essential accessories needed when using Cricut. After all, you can't cut without a blade.

Cutting blades also come in three types. First, we have the standard blade that usually accompanies the Cricut machine. The blade is very sharp and strong, but after a while, you will need to change the blade when it becomes blunt. So, you should have extra blades on hand just in case.

Next, we have the German carbide blade. You can easily purchase this from Cricut too. It's stronger than the standard blade, and it is created to cut through mid-weight materials. The blade also lasts for a longer time and doesn't easily break.

Lastly, designed for very thick materials, we have the deep-cut blade. The deep-cut blade is meant for cutting materials that go with the strong grip cutting mat. You can also use the blade to cut materials like stamp material, magnet, and some other fabrics.

- **Spatula and Scraper**

Not many people bother with purchasing a spatula and scraper when they want to use their Cricut machine. But these tools are useful when it comes to taking materials off the cutting mat.

For the spatula, you can use it to remove the material from the mat without damaging the material. It provides accuracy. In the case of the scraper, you will need to maintain the mat by cleaning it. This tool is helpful with scraping off leftover materials on the mat and cleaning it. This keeps the machine durable and it will last for a long time. Also, when you want to start a new project, you can quickly use the mat without having to clean it.

Apart from these essential tools, for specific types of projects, some devices are crucial when working on those projects.

Vinyl or Iron-On

For example, when working on vinyl or iron-on projects, they both use the same type of tools because they are both similar. Iron-on plans are pretty much heat transfer vinyl projects.

You can use vinyl to decorate tumblers, cups, or mugs; create decals for frames or walls and other projects. Iron-on is used to decorate fabric like adding designs on t-shirts.

- **Transfer Tape**

Cricut also manufactures this tool and it is entirely transparent. This way, when transferring or placing your vinyl project, you can see it easily and handle it more carefully.

- **Weeder**

When carrying out vinyl or iron-on projects, a weeder is crucial because it can be used to single out tiny pieces that are on your project like the pieces of vinyl that aren't being used from the backing sheet.

- **Paper**

Apart from vinyl projects, paper projects are probably the most popular projects that most crafters carry out. When using Cricut, most people start with paper projects because they are light and relatively more comfortable to do.

You can use paper to create shapes, numbers, letters, cards, envelopes, banners, decorations, stickers, and more. For paper projects, there are two general tools that you will possibly need.

- **Pens**

When using any of the Cricut Explore machines, you can quickly write out your designs. When you want to draw, Cricut provides some free fonts and some fonts that you can buy from Cricut Access. Also, if you have fonts on your computer, you can use that too.

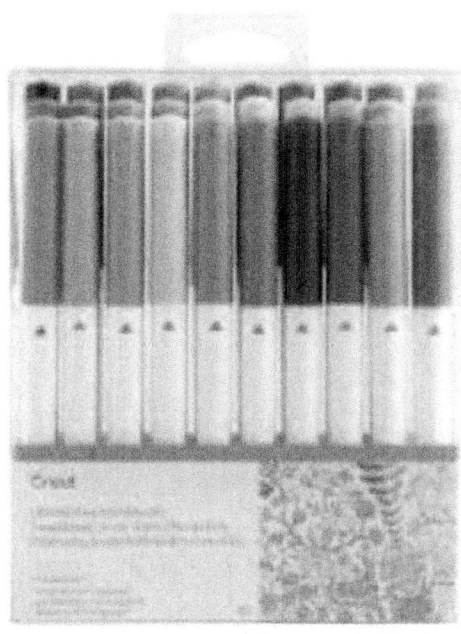

You can buy different pens from Cricut that are compatible with any of the Explore machines. Their types of pens include calligraphy pens, fine tip pens, gold pens, metallic pens, and pens of a wide range of colors. Although you can use other pens, Cricut machines work best with Cricut pens.

The great thing about Cricut machines is that they provide two slots so that you can use the pen and the blade simultaneously. This allows for quick designing and cutting instantaneously.

- **Scoring Tool**

This is also called a scoring stylus, and it is used for folding lines on boxes, envelopes, cards or any other paper. In the same way that you can design or draw and cut at the same time, you can also install the scoring tool in the machine when the blade is already installed.

This makes your designing process fast and easy.

Additional Tools

Apart from the usual design tools, you can also purchase some tools that make using the Cricut machine more convenient. Depending on the project you are using, these tools might be handy.

- **Tool Kit**

Instead of purchasing your tools one-by-one, some people go for the economical option and buy a tool kit. A standard tool kit should include scissors, weeders, scrapers, spatulas, and tweezers. If you're going into iron-on or vinyl projects, then you should probably purchase this type of tool kit.

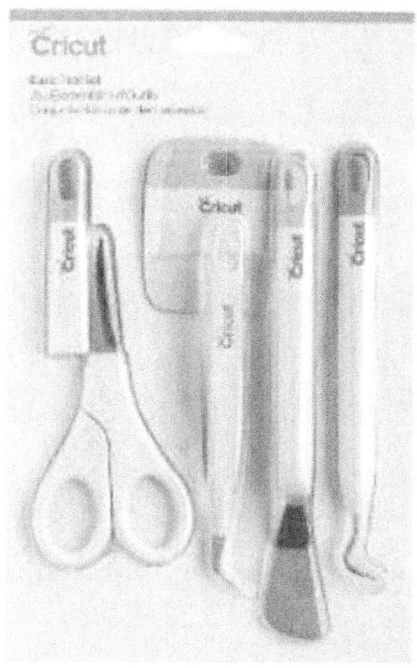

Some advanced tool kits add a paper trimmer and scoring stylus. This tool kit is excellent for those interested in paper projects.

- **Bluetooth Adapter**

Cricut Explore 1 does not come with an inbuilt Bluetooth adapter. If you want to use this model, you can buy a Bluetooth adapter from Cricut. This way, you can easily use your Cricut wherever your computer, laptop, or iPad is.

Chapter 4: The Materials Your Cricut Machine Needs

There are hundreds of different materials that can be worked on with Cricut machines. To be precise, Cricut machines can cut through many materials that are precisely or below 2.0 millimeters thickness. Users with Cricut Maker models have more cutting force and size advantage. The Cricut Maker model cuts ten times faster and can put up with materials that are up to 2.4 millimeters in thickness.

Many materials can be cut with a Cricut machine, even though the machine is mostly known for cutting paper or vinyl. The type of material to use depends solely on the type of objects you want to work with.

Main Materials

The type of materials you will choose for your cut will significantly depend on the kind of projects you want to engage in. Some of these materials work with different blades and can be used with more than one Cricut blade—this makes them be the essential materials associated with Cricut cutting and are the primary materials for your Cricut Explore machine.

To be more organized, we will mention some of them by category. You may be familiar with some of them as a beginner. However, you can pick up new materials from these categories and start trying them out on new projects.

Paper and Cardstock

It seems somewhat necessary to start with this category because they are the most popularly used class of material when designing. They have over thirty-five different kinds of materials under them, therefore making them the category with the highest number of resources.

Paper is another primary material you can use for cutting. You can make homemade greeting cards and envelopes from cutting paper with different designs. You can always choose from various types of paper from corrugated cardboard, kraft paper, foil, glitter paper, and many more.

Types of Paper or Cardboard

- Construction paper
- Cardstock
- Kraft board
- Metallic paper
- Copy paper

Transfer Tape

This is a clear, medium-strength adhesive tape that comes in sheets. This is an absolutely invaluable step of the process. We have some tips for you on getting the most out of your transfer tape and on choosing a transfer tape that will come in a quantity and power that is right for you and your projects.

I will tell you that the Cricut brand transfer tape comes in a single, rolled 12" x 48" sheet. You can cut pieces to your liking and use them multiple times before disposing of them. These sheets from Cricut are currently $8.99 at a local crafting retailer, while other brands offer a 12" roll of six to ten feet for a similar price.

While transfer tape is an absolutely integral part of the process of using your Cricut machine, the brand is not that important. Do some shopping around, find a sample size that works for you and your price point, and get started!

Like with any new type of crafting project, it will take some time to get used to the supplies and products, and to find the things that really work the best for you.

Now that a lot has been said about different types of materials that can be used on Cricut machines; you should be getting inspired to try out new different projects with these materials. However, only a beginner would stop here. We're not even close to unfolding the amazing parts of the usage of Cricut machines. You will get to know much later on in this book about the capabilities of Cricut machines and what you can do with them on an advanced level. Buckle up!

Vinyl

Professionals use vinyl materials a lot because they find them very effective and outstanding for making graphics, stencils, decals, signs, and so on. There are about 11 materials made from vinyl that can be used on Cricut machines.

Iron-On

This is also a vinyl product, but with a different framework. You can make use of this type of vinyl to design and decorate tote bags, t-shirts, caps, and other clothing items. There are around 9 iron-on materials that are used on Cricut machines.

Iron-on vinyl is also called heat transfer vinyl and one of the treasured materials to cut with Cricut Explore Air 2. You can use the iron-on vinyl to design bags, t-shirts, and any other items.

Types of Iron-on

- Printable iron-on
- Glossy iron-on
- Metallic iron-on
- Foil iron-on

Fabric and Textiles

Fabrics are naturals on Cricut machines; they work seamlessly on almost every Cricut machine model. There are about 17 different materials under this category. However, most of the time, they need stabilizers to be added before cutting.

Textile or Fabric is not an unusual material for some Cricut users, but because the variety of fabric available to choose from is so vast, it needs to be mentioned again because there are some techniques and materials that are a little more unusual. For example, cutting a lace-like pattern into fabrics can immediately add a color palette of fancy lace to any project. This also makes it possible to have the same lace pattern on a variety of complimentary fabrics or colors.

There is a fabric blade that is specific to the fabric material; all you need to do is to keep the fabric set in place on the settings dial. Cricut has some fabric materials online that you can cut with.

Types of Fabric

- Leather
- Canvas
- Duck cloth
- Silk
- Linen

Infusible Ink

Infusible ink is an exciting material from Cricut that allows heat transfer on white and light-colored materials. It comes in different colors, patterns, and gradients and is designed to be resistant to peeling, flaking and washing. It can be used for shirts, totes, coasters, etc.

Other Materials

Apart from all these five categories of materials we have discussed, there are several other unique materials that can also be used on Cricut machines. Ranging from by-products of foils, woods, sheets, board, Bellum, chips, tapes to many other natural and artificial resources, there are at least 30 of them that can be worked on by Cricut machines. There are materials that people think are not compatible with Cricut machines. Well, you'd be surprised.

Faux Leather and Leather

Depending on your preference, you can use either material. Despite what you choose, both are good materials to cut with the Cricut. Custom jewelry, like necklace pendants or earrings, is simple and stunning projects. These make beautiful and personal gifts or add the right touch to a special outfit. Leather can also be used for making fashionable bracelets or cuffs.

Having an intricate cut on a lovely piece of leather or faux leather, the bracelet can be attached to an adjustable band. Hair bows or bows to add to clothing or handbags are also possible. For a hair bow, glue a hair clip to the back when the bow is finished. Use hot glue or another adhesive to attach the bow to clothing or a purse. Other hair accessories can be made, like flowers and other shapes.

These can be attached to hair clips, like the bows, or attached to hard or stretchy headbands. Leather can also be used as an embellishment to pillows or other fabrics, like chair backs, or made into manly coasters.

Felt

Felt is another multi-functional material that you can use for a host of projects. Because this item is fairly sturdy but has good flexibility, it is perfect for just about anything.

In addition, it comes in all different colors and is relatively inexpensive. Some unique projects that can be made from felt include garlands of multi-layered flowers to hang over a window curtain or above a bed, a textured phrase attached to a pillow, an interactive tree-shaped advent calendar, banners, ornaments, and cupcake or cake toppers.

Chapter 5: How Will You Use Your Cricut Machine? The Setting of Cricut Machine

So, you have all your materials on hand, which is awesome, but how do you actually use a Cricut machine? Well, that's what you're about to find out. If looking at your Cricut machine makes you feel confused, then continue reading—here, we'll tell you how to use your new Cricut machine in a simple, yet effective way.

Setting up the Machine

First, you'll want to set up the Cricut machine. To begin, create a space for it. A craft room is the best place for this, but if you're at a loss of where to put it, I suggest setting it up in a dining room if possible. Make sure you have an outlet nearby or a reliable extension cord.

Next, read the instructions. Often, you can jump right in and begin using the equipment, but with Cricut machines, it can be very tedious. The best thing to do is to read all the materials you get with your machine.

Make sure that you do have ample free space around the machine itself, because you will be loading mats in and out and you'll need that little bit of wiggle room.

The next thing to set up is, of course, the computer where the designs will be created. Make sure that whatever medium you're using has an internet connection, since you'll need to download the Cricut Design Space app. If it's a machine earlier than the Explore Air 2, it will need to be plugged in directly, but if it's a wireless machine like the Air 2, you can simply link this up to your computer, and from there, design what you need to design.

Using Cricut Software

So, Cricut machines use a program called Cricut Design Space, and you'll need to make sure that you have this downloaded and installed when you're ready. Download the app if you plan to use a smartphone or tablet, or if you're on the computer, go to http://design.cricut.com/setup to get the software. If it's not hooked up already, make sure you've got Bluetooth compatibility enabled on the device, or the cord plugged in. To turn on your machine, hold the power button. You'll then go to settings, where you should see your Cricut model in Bluetooth settings. Choose that, and from there, your device will ask you to put a Bluetooth passcode in. Just make this something generic and easy to remember.

Once that's done, you can now use Design Space.

So, what I love about Design Space is that it's incredibly easy to use. They know you're a beginner, so you'll notice it's very easy to navigate.

Now, I personally like to use the app for Design Space, since this will allow you to have every design uploaded to the cloud so that you can reuse your designs. However, if you want to use them without having an internet connection, you'll want to make sure that you download them and save them to the device itself, rather than relying on the cloud.

When you're in the online mode, you'll see a lot of projects that you can use. For the purpose of this tutorial, I do suggest making sure that you choose an easy one, such as the "Enjoy Card" project you can get automatically.

So, you've got everything linked up—let's move onto the first cut for this project.

Imputing Cartridges and Keypad

The first cut that you'll be doing involves keypad input and cartridges, and these are usually done with the "Enjoy Card" project you get right away. So, once everything is set up, choose this project, and from there, you can use the tools and the accessories within the project.

You will need to set the smart dial before you get started making your projects. This is on the right side of the Explore Air 2, and it's basically the way you choose your materials. Turn the dial to whatever type of material you want, since this helps with ensuring you've got the right blade settings. There are even half settings for those in-between projects.

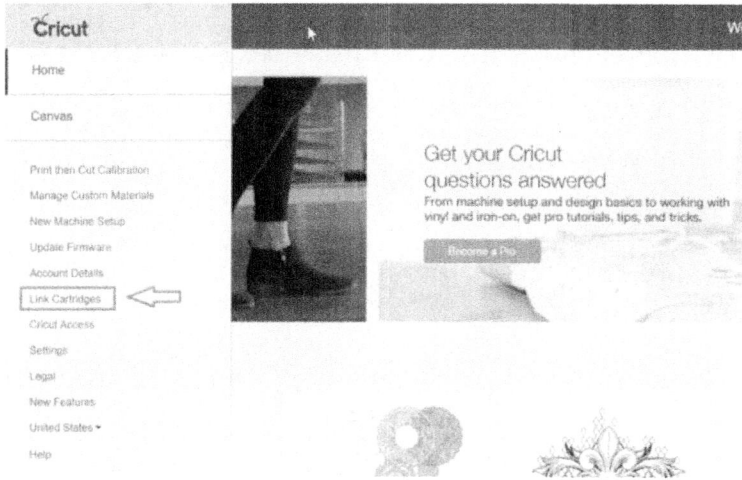

For example, let's say you have some light cardstock. You can choose that setting, or the adjacent half setting. Once this is chosen in Design Space, your machine will automatically adjust to the correct setting.

You can also choose the fast mode, which is in the "set, load, go" area on the screen, and you can then check the position of the box under the indicator for dial position. Then, press this and make your cut. However, the fast mode is incredibly loud, so be careful.

Now, we've mentioned cartridges. While these usually aren't used in the Explore Air 2 machines anymore, they are helpful with beginner projects. To do this, once you have the Design Space software and everything is connected, go to the hamburger menu and you'll see an option called "ink cartridges." Press that bad boy, and from there, choose the Cricut device. The machine will then tell you to put your cartridge in. Do that, and once it's detected, it will tell you to link the cartridge.

Remember, though, that once you link this, you can't use it with other machines—the one limit to these cartridges.

Once it's confirmed, you can go to images, and click the cartridges option to find the ones that you want to make. You can filter the cartridges to figure out what you need, and you can check out your images tab for any other cartridges that are purchased or uploaded.

You can get digital cartridges, which means you buy them online and choose the images directly from your available options. They aren't physical, so there is no linking required.

Loading and Unloading Your Paper

To load paper into a Cricut machine, you'll want to make sure that the paper is at least three inches by three inches. Otherwise, it won't cut very well. You should use regular paper for this.

Now, to make this work, you need to put the paper onto the cutting mat. You should have one of those, so take it right now and remove the attached film. Put a corner of the paper to the area where you are directed to align the paper corners. From there, push the paper directly onto the cutting mat for proper adherence. Once you do that, you just load it into the machine, following the arrows. You'll want to keep the paper firmly on the mat. Press the "load paper" key that you see as you do this. If it doesn't take for some reason, press the unload paper key, and try this again until it shows up.

Now, before you do any cutting for your design, you should always have a test cut in place. Some people don't do this, but it's incredibly helpful when learning how to use a Cricut. Otherwise, you won't get the correct pressure in some cases, so get in the habit of doing it for your pieces.

Is there a difference between vinyl and other products? The primary difference is the cutting mats. Depending on what you're cutting, you may need some grip or lack thereof. If you feel like your material isn't fully sticking, get some Heat N' Bond to help with this since often the issue with cutting fabrics comes from the fact that it doesn't adhere. But you may also need mats that are a bit thicker, too, to help get a better grip on these.

Selecting Shapes, Letters, and Phrases

When you're creating your design in Design Space, you usually begin by using letters, shapes, numbers, or different fonts. These are the basics and they're incredibly easy.

To make text, you just press the text tool on the left-hand side and type out your text. For example, write the word hello, or joy, or whatever you want to use.

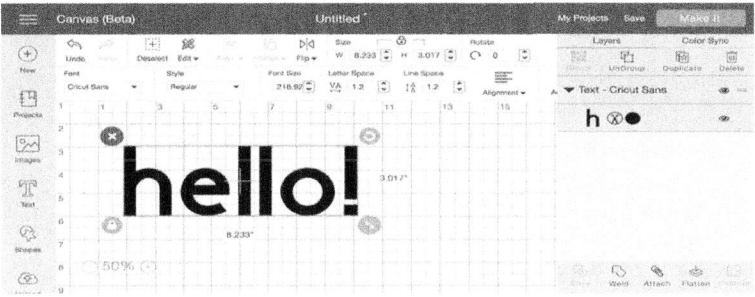

You can change the font size by pressing the drag and drop arrow near the corner of the text box, or by going to the size panel near the top to choose actual font sizes. You can also choose different Cricut or system fonts, too. Cricut ones will be in green, and if you have Cricut Access, this is a great way to begin using this. You can also sort them, so you don't end up accidentally paying for a font.

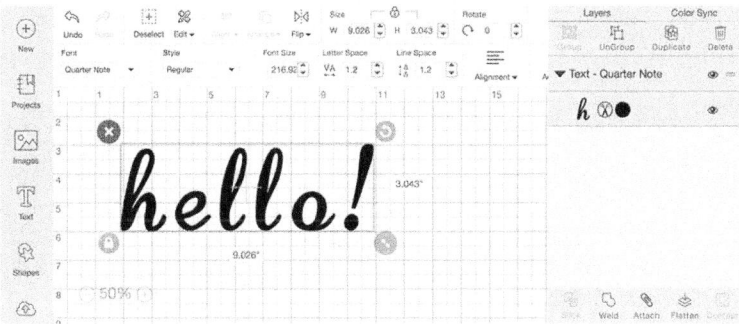

The Cricut ones are supposed to be made for Cricut, so you know they'll look good. Design Space also lets you put them closer together so they can be cut with a singular cut. You can change this by going to line spacing and adjusting as needed. To fix

67

certain letters, you go to the drop-down advanced menu to ungroup the letters, so everything is separate as needed.

Cricut also offers different writing styles, which is a great way to add text to projects. The way to do this is to choose a font that's made with a specific style and choose only the Cricut ones, and then go to writing. This will then narrow down the choice so you're using a good font for writing.

Adding shapes is pretty easy, as well. In Design Space, choose the shapes option. Once you click it, the window will then pop out, and you'll have a wonderful array of different shapes that you can use with just one click. Choose your shape, and from there, put it in the space. Drag the corners in order to make this bigger or smaller.

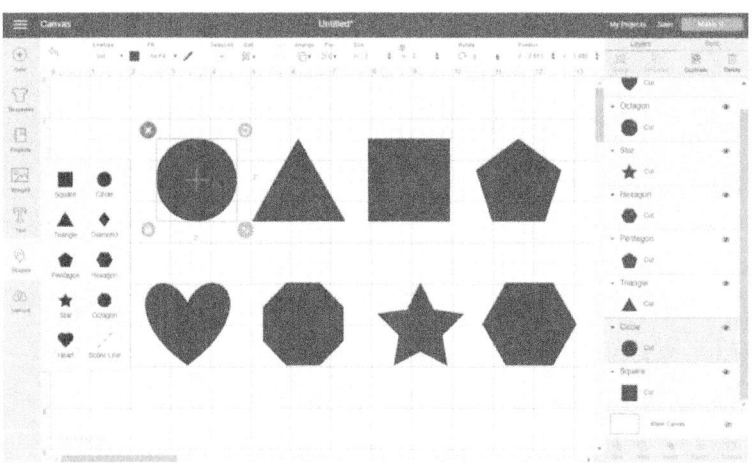

There is also the scoreline, which creates a folding line for you to use. Personally, if you're thinking of trying to make a card at first, I suggest using this.

You can also resize your options by dragging them towards the right-hand side, and you can change the orientation by choosing that option and then flipping it around. You can select exact measurements as well, which is good for those design projects that need everything to be precise.

Once you've chosen the design, it's time for you to start cutting, and we'll discuss this next step below.

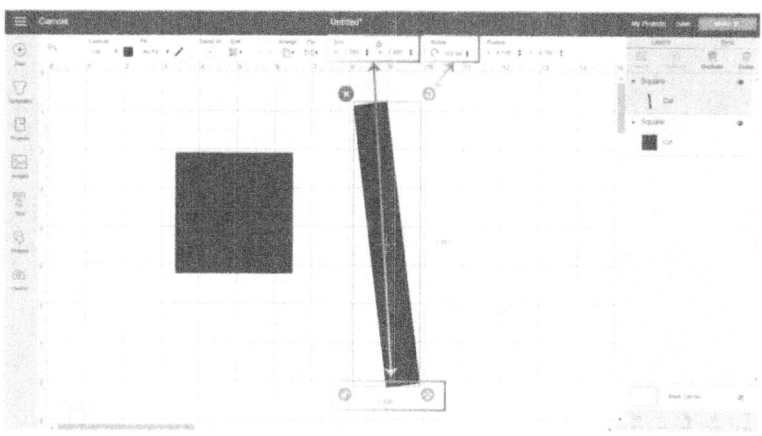

How to Remove Your Cut from the Cutting Mat

Removing your cut from the mat is easy, but complicated. Personally, I ran into the issue of it being more complicated with vinyl projects since they love to just stick around there. But we'll explain how you can create great cuts and remove them, as well.

Techniques for Cricut Cartridges

On the off chance that you've been a piece of the general Cricut fever that keeps on clearing the country, at that point you've without a doubt been satisfied that you're never again compelled to pay the first high costs as when Cricut cartridges were at first discharged. The Lite Cupcake Wrappers cartridge isn't a special case to this standard.

The Cupcake Wrappers Cartridge Itself

Maybe you have recognized it from the name, and this particular cartridge is a piece of the 'Light' collection. The Lite cartridges have immediately ended up being highly supported since their underlying uncovering. Not exclusively do a great deal of them fill in explicit cartridge topic holes inside the full cartridge gathering, but having unadulterated substance material and significantly less of the generally squandered additional items, they likewise make sense to be a mess progressively moderate.

The Lite Cupcake Wrappers cartridge was made for each cake (and particularly cupcake) dough punchers around. The round is packaged with 50 unique cupcake holders or wrapper pictures that you're ready to pick and remove to hold your newly prepared cupcake. The arrangement likewise offers a little decision of cupcake topper decorations, which are perfect for fixing off your definitive handcrafted cupcake.

You must love exactly how making every cupcake wrapper is presently so natural and fast, and the completed visual effect is cute. When you start to utilize this cartridge to adorn most of your handcrafted cupcakes, trust me, not simply will an old 'stripped' cake in a flash end up being amazingly uninteresting. Yet, you will search out chances to heat cakes for any event to get every one of the compliments from everyone that sees them.

The Designs and Sizes

Pictures for cupcake wrapper structures vacillate between fragile, for all intents and purposes doily looking examples to increasingly contemporary styles, alongside a few models that incorporate valuable words and expressions, so there is surely a unique format to suit each cupcake occasion.

One of the most constant inquiries in regards to this particular cartridge is concerning the size. The wrapper structures can be cut in size to oblige any size cupcake (sensibly speaking, obviously), yet be admonished that you may need to rehearse on more than one occasion before transforming into a specialist with what measurements your machine should be set to about the particular cupcake boundary. The uplifting news is you'll undoubtedly have the option to get the hang of it in a brief timeframe.

Undertaking Ideas

Normally, if you're just preparing a lot of cupcakes to expend yourself, you doubtlessly won't have any desire to utilize this cartridge. However, for each other event, it is, without a doubt, an unquestionable requirement to change over fundamental cupcakes into a touch of something unique. Loads of individuals utilize this specific cartridge to spruce up the standard cupcakes served at kids' parties. For social events, anyway, anyplace a cake or two is discovered, the Lite Cupcake Wrapper cartridge can make every one of them simply significantly more exceptional.

Tips on How to Ensure Its Longevity

First of all, ensure that you secure it consistently. When you are finished utilizing it, place a spread over your tangle. Clear plastic can support a major ordeal. On the off chance that you have two mats, you utilize both to cover each other from eye to eye. Likewise, clear out any abundance of paper that is deserted on the floor covering. You can do this by utilizing child wipes. In any case, if your Cricut mats have just exceeded their normal life regardless of genuine endeavors on your part to look after them, you can utilize a knitting splash to recover its stickiness.

Cartridges are an ongoing discussion among Cricut users for a variety of reasons.

A cartridge is what contains the images and fonts that you'll be cutting. Most cartridges hold 700 or 800 images. Lite cartridges contain about 50 images and have one or two creative features. Despite the limitations, you can still be creative and produce hundreds of variations with this less expensive choice.

You usually receive at least one cartridge with the purchase of your machine. Sometimes this is preloaded into your machine as a digital cartridge. You may buy downloadable digital cartridges online for immediate use, or you can buy the physical plastic cartridges that you slide into your machine.

When you purchase a cartridge, you can use that physical cartridge in your machine, or you also have the option to link that cartridge to the Cricut Craft Room (CCR).

The Craft Room allows you to view your images on your computer screen, making it easier to see and manipulate your projects.

By linking to CCR, you won't have to bother to switch out your cartridges physically. If you plan ever to sell the cartridges, then do not link them. Once they are linked, you are not legally allowed to sell them. This is understandable. Some people might link them to the Craft Room, so they have access to the images and then sell the physical cartridge.

To link your cartridges, you'll need to do the following. Load the cartridge you want to add to your machine. Go online to the Craft Room. Under all cartridges, select my cartridges. You will see a list of cartridges. Find the cartridge you want to add and click Link and follow the prompts.

Another advantage of adding your cartridges to the Craft Room is that you'll be able to pull images from several cartridges to use at one time. When you're using the physical cartridge, you can only use images from one cartridge at a time.

If you buy a used cartridge, you need to ask if it's linked. If it is, you will still be able to use the physical cartridge in your machine, but you will not be able to link it to the Craft Room. A cartridge can only be linked once. It is still possible to use the cartridge in the Craft Room, but you can't link it. You'll have to have the physical cartridge in your machine to cut the images.

It is now possible to purchase cartridges online and download them to your account. This means you don't have to wait for a physical cartridge to arrive in the mail. You have immediate access to the images. These are the digital cartridges that I referred to earlier.

Many people complain that the cartridges are too expensive. Instead of spending $80 on a cartridge with hundreds of images, many people would prefer to be able to buy an image they want for one dollar or two; that's where single images or sets come into play.

You can buy single digital images or smaller sets for a fraction of the cost of a full cartridge. You can even rent cartridge bundles for 30 days on a monthly subscription on the Cricut home page under the shopping section.

Make sure you take advantage of the free cartridges offered in the Craft Room. The only thing to remember is to finish your projects.

Once the cartridge is no longer free, you will not be able to cut your image.

You can save money on cartridges watching for sales and special promotions.

It is possible to share physical cartridges with friends. This is good if they want a few images for a special project, but don't plan to use the cartridge enough to justify buying it.

Digital Handbooks for Easy Reference

Did you know you can download the digital handbook of any cartridge and save it as a PDF file on your computer? Just go to Cricut.com, click on the shop, images, and cartridges. Select any cartridge, click on it scrolling down the page till you see the link for the digital handbook, open it and save it to your hard drive for easy reference.

Sharing Cut Files

A cut file is a project that someone has already created and laid out on their Cricut. They saved the file and shared it on their blog or in the Craft Room. What this does is prevent you from re-creating the wheel.

If you see a project you like, you can save the file onto your computer. Then go to the Craft Room and import that file. You can then make the same cuts without having to figure out how to lay everything out. The images are already sized and laid out for you.

The advantage of this is you can save yourself a lot of time by using layouts that others have already created.

But here's the tricky part, you must already own the cartridges the images are from. You can't make the cuts if you don't own the cartridges the images originated from.

You can also save your projects and share them in the Craft Room for others to use.

When you see a cute project on Pinterest or a craft blog, you might want to ask if the cut file is available and, if so, what cartridges it uses.

Organization

If you're like most crafters, including me, you'll eventually become overrun with craft "stuff." You'll have paper stacks, vinyl rolls, and other material that you're planning to use someday spread all over your craft area.

Your cartridges may be lying around in a pile, and you have to spend twenty minutes searching every time you need a specific overlay or booklet.

Eventually, this creates such a feeling of chaos and frustration that you dread going into your Craft Room or crafting area.

This can all be solved with some organization. It may take you a few hours to get it all in order, but it will save you countless hours in the future. You'll no longer feel depressed every time you look at your crafting space.

Craft stores will often have storage containers specially made for certain types of crafts. But you may want to start at your local chain stores. They often have craft and office supply departments where you can find storage units cheaply.

You can find containers where you can sort all your paper into small shelves based on color and type of paper. If you don't like the ones at the craft store, then try an office supply store. If you live in an extremely humid area, you may want to store your paper in plastic containers.

Another option is to watch for garage sales that say "craft items." Many people spend hundreds of dollars getting set up for a particular craft and then discover they don't have the time or inclination to spend much time doing the craft. This can be a bonanza for other crafters.

Photo boxes can be used to keep your booklets and overlays safe and organized.

Some crafters copy their overlays, laminate them and bind them together on rings where they can easily be added or removed.

There are special carrying cases, binders, and totes designed just for cartridges.

The first thing to remember is to make sure that you're using the right mat. The light grip ones are good for very light material, with the pink one being one of the strongest, and only to be used with the Cricut Maker. Once the design is cut, you'll probably be eager McBeaver about removing the project directly from the mat, but one of the problems with this is that often, the project will be ruined if you're not careful. Instead of pulling the project from the mat itself, bend the mat within your hand, and push it away from the project, since this will loosen it from the mat. Bend this both

79

horizontally and vertically, so that the adhesive releases the project.

Do you remember the spatula tool that we told you to get with your Cricut machine early on? This is where you use it. Use this spatula to lightly pull on the vinyl, until you can grab it from the corner and lift it up. Otherwise, you risk curling it or tearing the mat, which is what we don't want.

Now, with the initial cuts, such as the paper ones, this will be incredibly easy. Trust me, I was surprised at how little effort it took, but one of the biggest things to remember is that with Cricut machines, you have to go slow when removing the material. Do this slowly, and don't get rushed near the end. Taking your time will save you a lot of problems, and it will even save you money and stress, too!

You will notice that Cricut mats are incredibly sticky, and if you don't have a Cricut spatula on hand or don't want to spend the money, metal spatulas will work too. You can put the paper on a flat surface and then lightly remove it. But always be careful when removing these items.

Cricut machines are pretty easy to use, and the beauty is that with the right understanding and ideas, you can make any items you want to.

Chapter 6: Maintenance of the Machine

The Cricut Cutter machine needs to be kept intact in a variety of ways: the blade must be replaced, the cutting mats must be taken care of, and the machine, in general, must be kept clean.

Cutting Blade

Every single blade you use might get up to fifteen thousand individual cuts before it needs to be replaced. To prolong this number of individual cuts, place the aluminum foil onto the cutting mat and cut out a few designs. This process keeps the blade extra sharp and lengthens the life of the blade. This number of cuts can be greatly based on the types of materials that have been cut by the blade. If you are doing many projects in which thick materials need to be cut, the blade will deteriorate quickly; the blade can also deteriorate quickly if you are cutting many materials under high pressure. A good way to know if your blade needs to be replaced is if the quality of your cuts starts to greatly decrease. If this happens, it's best to replace the cutting blade. When replacing the blade, it is always best to get blades that are Cricut brand. Generic blades are often not the best quality and will cause you to constantly replace your cutting blade. To install the new blade once, you've ordered the correct one, you need to first unplug your Cricut Cutter machine. Always unplug the machine before installing anything in your Cricut cutter. Next, you must remove the old, dull cutting blade from your Cricut Cutter machine. Once the cutting blade assembly has been separated, it is now time to eject the blade. Find the small silver button above the adjustment knob and press the button down; this will eject the cutting blade. Be very, very careful when doing this as the blade is extremely sharp and can easily cut through the skin. Keep all blades away from children and pets. To put in the new blade, insert the blade into the end of the blade assembly opposite the blade release button. The blade will then be pulled up into the assembly.

Subscribe to Cricut Access

If you really want to get a full range of use out of both your Cricut Explore machine as well as the Cricut Maker machine, we would recommend you subscribe to Cricut Access right away. There are two options for payment. You can either pay a monthly fee of $10, or you can pay once for the entire year. This works out to be slightly cheaper on a month-to-month basis. This will give you access to thousands of different predesigned projects as well as Cricut Access exclusive fonts, that you would otherwise have to pay to use. If you are planning to use your Cricut a lot, this will save you a lot of money as opposed to buying an image for every project individually. We can all agree it is a lot easier to pay one flat rate instead of having to figure out how much you are spending on projects. Get your money's worth out of your Cricut and subscribe to Cricut Access.

De-tack Your Cutting Mat

The Cricut Explore machine will come with a green 12"x12" standard grip cutting mat. The Cricut Maker machine will come with a blue light grip mat. As you already know, you will place your cutting material onto this mat before inserting it into the machine to cut. As you will come to find out, the green cutting mat is extremely sticky when it is brand new.

Keep Your Cutting Mat Covers

The cutting mats that you purchase for your projects will always come brand new with a plastic protecting sheet over them. This can be pulled off and put back on for the entire life of the mat. You will want to keep this plastic cover if you have the mat. It will keep the stickiness level up on your mat, and it will make the mat easier to store away when not in use.

Cutting Mat

The Cutting mat in addition to the cutting blade needs to be taken care of. One cutting mat can have a life of anywhere from twenty-five to forty cuts. The life of the cutting mat can vary from this amount depending on the pressure and speed at which the cuts have been made and the type of materials that have been cut on the mat. To prolong the life of your cutting mat, remove any debris from the mat after a cut and always avoid scraping the mat. If you scrape the mat, it can push any debris further into the mat. After each craft, it is best to run lukewarm water over the mat and dab it dry with a towel afterward. When a material can no longer adhere to the cutting mat, then it is time to finally replace the mat. It is recommended to get many cutting mats and rotate between them to prolong the life of all the cutting mats. This extends the life of the mats because one cutting mat will not be cut on for many, many projects in a small amount of time. It is also recommended that you keep all your cutting mats and all your cartridges and blades in a very organized manner. Throwing the components haphazardly can destroy and deteriorate them, so it is best to keep them in a very organized way. A benefit of keeping your Cricut Cutter components organized is that you won't lose or damage the very expensive items that are necessary for several projects.

How to Clean a Cricut Mat

Sometimes it also depends on the materials you use that make your machine dirty. For example, using felt means you'd need to grab stray pieces using tweezers. Another great way to clean your Cricut machine is to use a lint roller across the entire machine to pick up debris, scrap vinyl, and pieces of felt. You can also use this roller on your mats.

To clean your mats, if there is any leftover residue on your mats, the general rule is to use bleach and alcohol-free baby wipes to gently wipe the mat clean and remove it from grime, glue, and dust. You can also get yourself GOO GONE. Spray this on your mat and let it sit for 15 minutes, then use a scraper tool to remove the adhesive. But do this only if your mat is very dirty. Otherwise, wet wipes will do.

Another tip to keep your mats clean is by putting a protective cover back over them when you are not using them.

Cleaning the Cricut Machine

The final thing to keep clean is the actual Cricut Cutter machine. The machine needs to be wiped down with a damp cloth. Only wipe down the external panels of the machine and with the machine unplugged. Always wipe down the machine with a dry cloth after cleaning the outside of the machine. Never clean the Cricut Cutter machine with abrasive cleaners such as acetone, benzene, and all other alcohol-based cleaners. Abrasive cleaning tools should also not be used on the Cricut Cutter machine. In addition, never submerge any component of the machine or the Cricut Cutter machine into the water, as it can damage the machine. Always keep the Cricut Cutter machine away from all foods, liquids, pets, and children. Keep the Cricut Cutter machine in a very dry and dust-free environment. Finally, do not put the Cricut Cutter machine in excessive heat, excessive cold, sunlight, or any area where the plastic or any other components on the Cricut Cutter machine can melt.

Ensure Your Machine Is on Stable Footing

This may seem pretty basic, but ensuring that your machine is on a level surface will allow it to make more precise cuts every single time. Rocking the machine or wobbling could cause unstable results in your projects.

Ensure no debris has gotten stuck under the feet of your machine that could cause instability before proceeding to the next troubleshooting step!

Redo all Cable Connections

So your connections are in the best possible working order, undo all your cable connections, blow into the ports or use canned air, and then securely plug everything back into the right ports. This will help to make sure all the connections are communicating with each other where they should be!

Completely Dust and Clean Your Machine

Your little Cricut works hard for you! Return the favor by making sure you're not allowing gunk, dust, grime, or debris to build up in the surfaces and crevices. Adhesive can build up on the machine around the mat input and on the rollers, so be sure to focus on those areas!

Check Your Blade Housing

Sometimes debris and leavings from your materials can build up inside the housings for your blades! Open them up and clear any built-up materials that could be impeding swiveling or motion.

Sharpen Your Blades

A very popular Cricut trick in use is to stick a clean, fresh piece of foil to your Cricut mat, and run it through with the blade you wish to sharpen. Running the blades through the thin metal helps to revitalize their edges and give them a little extra staying power until it's time to buy replacements.

Chapter 7: Tips and Tricks on How to Start and How to Make Your First Project

While Cricut's website offers many tips and techniques, there are some tried-and-true ways of using your machine and saving money and time.

10 Top Tips and Tactics for Success

1. Freezer paper is ideal for creating custom stencils.
2. Label blades for use on paper, vinyl, fabric, etc., only use those blades on that medium. It helps preserve the lifetime of the edges.
3. Learn the proper cutting methods and approved materials by reading the cutting guide on Cricut.com.
4. Spray paint is an excellent tool for coloring vinyl if you are ever in a hurry and do not have a required color on hand or the time for it to arrive.

5. Free fonts can be uploaded and used in the Cricut Design Space. Find free fonts on websites such as dafont.com, fontsquirrel.com, or 1001freefonts.com.

6. Personal images and pictures can be used for Cricut projects if the image is saved on the computer as a PNG, JPG, or SCG.

7. Test out materials before printing and cutting a final project to be sure it will work as planned.

8. Pens other than Cricut pens work with the machine. Some brands to try include Sharpie, American Crafts and Recollections.

9. Avoid paper curling by pulling the cutting mat from the project and not the other way around.

10. Lint rollers are great for removing leftover materials from cutting mats. If the carpets need further cleaning, use soap and water and gently rub clean with a soft cloth. Rinse with clean water and let air dry.

Cutting with Your Cricut

Masking tape or painter's tape is excellent to place on the edges of materials when they do not stick well to the cutting mat.

Thick cuts sometimes will not be cut completely. To avoid having to do it by hand, keep the material in place when it finishes cutting the first cut without pressing the arrows button to remove it and then cut it again by selecting the "Go" or "C" button.

Print and Cut

An inkjet printer works best for printing. A laser printer sometimes heats the toner too high, making it hard for the Cricut machine to read.

Internet Explorer or Safari is best for working with large images because these browsers support about 9 inches high and about 6 inches wide. Chrome and Firefox cap their heights around 8 inches tall and about 5 inches wide.

A white paper is best for printing the registration marks for projects. If the project is any other color, print and cut on white paper first, attach them to the colored paper before putting it into the Cricut.

Writing with Your Cricut

Pens work best when stored cap-side down. It keeps the ink at the tip.

Thin pens can have their barrel widened by winding tape around them. The electrical or painter's tape works well and does not leave a sticky residue behind.

Scoring with Your Cricut

Folding materials are made more comfortable using the scoring tool when placed in the machine's pen holder.

Deepen the score lines in a custom design by doubling up the canvas's score lines in the Design Space.

Embossing with Your Cricut

It can do! Use the accessory adapter in the place of the blade housing and insert the scoring stylus into it. When the Cricut tells of cutting, it will emboss instead.

Badges for Your Cricut

Sharpen blades with aluminum foil by cutting a basic design into the foil on the cutting mat.

Designing for Your Cricut

Firefox and Safari are best for using Design Space. Google Chrome does not work well with it.

Save the free designs that Design Space offers by saving a new project with the design and name it with a design description for easy access.

Cut the canvas exactly how it is laid out by selecting "All" and clicking on "Attach." It ensures everything stays where it is without the machine defaulting to individual cuts.

Instructional handbooks are available for Cricut Access members. This link is a functional place to learn how to assemble cartridges. (www.home.cricut.com/handbooks)

Cut the most massive layer last to avoid the material from moving around during the smaller cuts. It means placing the most massive layer as the topmost layer and the more delicate elements at the bottom in Design Space.

Chapter 8: FAQ for Cricut

What Is a Cricut?

A Cricut is a machine that you can use for cutting a variety of different art projects. It is a machine designed to speed up the crafting process and help you make professional and homemade crafts in the comfort of your own home.

Where Can I Download the Software for the Explore Machines?

You can go to design.cricut.com and use your Cricut ID to log in. This process is relatively easy and anyone comfortable enough to download things from the computer will be able to do this. Even if you have never downloaded anything before, the website will prompt you to download Design Space and everything after that will be guided as well.

Where Can I Download the Software If I Am on Mobile?

If you are on iOS, you have to go to the App Store and search for the Cricut Design Space app. If you are on Android, simply go to

Google Play and search for the same thing. All you have to do is download it like any other app, log in, and you are ready to use Design Space.

What Are the Differences between the Machines?

The Cricut Explore 1 does not have Bluetooth and will need a Cricut Wireless Bluetooth Adapter to use with your mobile. The Cricut Maker, Explore Air and Explore Air 2 all have built-in Bluetooth.

The Cricut Explore 1 also has a single Carriage, which means that it cannot multitask like the Explore Air, Cricut Maker, and Explore Air 2.

The Explore Air 2 comes in different colors and cuts faster than the Explore Air and the Cricut Explore 1.

Cricut Maker has storage space and can cut through thicker materials.

Does My Machine Come with a Carry Bag of Sorts?

No, it does not. A carry bag can be purchased from the store, but it is incredibly overpriced. What's the use of having a Cricut if you can't make your own carry bag?

Writing and Scoring, Can I Do It?

Yes, you can. With the Cricut Maker, Explore Air and Explore Air 2, you can either write and cut or score and cut at the same time. The Cricut Explore 1 can do all of it too, but not at the same time.

Is the Design Space the Same for Both the Cricut Maker and the Explore?

Yes, it is. Long story short; it is exactly the same.

Does the Cricut Maker Have Fast Mode?

Yes, it does. It has a setting for up to 2x faster than normal.

What Is the Thickest My Cutting Materials Can Be for the Cricut Explore Machines?

The Explore machines can cut materials up to 2mm, but nothing thicker.

What Is the Thickest My Cutting Materials Can Be for the Cricut Maker?

The Cricut Maker can cut materials up to 2.5mm, which doesn't sound like much, but it makes a huge difference.

Do I Need the Internet?

Yes and no. When you are on a desktop, there is no offline option for Design Space. However, if you are on mobile, the app will allow you to work offline and you won't need the Internet for any of it.

Can Design Space Work on More Than One Device?

Yes. Design Space works with the cloud and not a specific device. This means that anything with access to the cloud can access your account and use your Cricut machine without any hassle.

How Long Do Images I Have Purchased Stay in My Possession?

Images do not expire once you have purchased them. They stay yours forever.

Why Is My Material Tearing All the Time and What Can I Do to Stop It?

There are many reasons why your materials might be tearing. It could be that you are not using the right settings, your blade is too blunt, the design that you are trying to cut is too intricate and you need to make it larger or cut slower. There are more possibilities, though. You could be using the wrong blade for your crafts or your materials just aren't working well enough with your Cricut Maker and you might want to invest in better materials in the future. Your mat may also be too sticky or too loose.

Are My Old Blades Compatible with the Cricut Maker?

Yes, they are. The Cricut Maker is compatible with old accessories and tools, as well as new ones that will be released in the future.

How Do I Change the Blades and Accessories?

For the blades, you can merely open the clamp marked with a B and remove the blade housing. Now you have an empty clamp and you won't be able to do anything without another blade in the clamp.

To replace the blade in the housing, all you have to do is remove the blade carefully so you don't cut yourself, remove the protective cover from the new blade, and put that in the new housing just like the one you took out. There is a magnet in the housing that keeps the blades in place. All that's left is to return the housing to the clamp and you will be ready to go.

For the accessories, you want to open the clamp and slide the accessory adapter out. Do this by pushing it upward from below. Add your accessory and put it back in the clamp.

The Cricut Explore 1 only has one clamp, which means you will have to switch between the accessory adapter and blade housing. It changes nothing about the process of replacing the blades and accessories. The only difference is that both use the same clamp.

Do I Need a Printer to Use My Cricut?

In a word, no. Using your Cricut doesn't require ink from a printer, though there are some materials on the market for Cricut, which are specifically meant to be printed on before using.

If you're not using these items, then you will find that you can get the most out of your machine without that feature.

If you wish to print things then cut them, this is known as the Print then Cut method and there is a wealth of knowledge about this on the internet. You can make iron-on decals, tattoos, and so much more!

Chapter 9: Cricut Dictionary

When working with the Cricut cutting machines and Design Space, you are going to come across different terminology. The following is a glossary of the Cricut vocabulary to help you better understand the system. The following are general Cricut terminology as "Design Space" terminology.

Backing

The backing is the back sheet of a material such as vinyl. It is the part of the material that gets stuck onto the cutting mat and is usually the last part of the material to be removed after cutting, weeding, and transfer of the project.

Bleed

The bleed refers to a space around each item to be cut. This gives the cutting machine the ability to make a more precise cut. It is a small border that separates cutting items on a page. This option can be turned off, but it is not recommended.

Bonded Fabric

Bonded fabric is a material that is not very elastic, it is held together with adhesive and is not typical woven type fabric.

If there is some gunk visible on the blade, pinch around the blade shaft using a very careful grip with your opposite thumb and forefinger, and bring it back, making sure you don't go against the blade angle as you do. This will remove any foreign material from your blade tip and make your cuts more accurate.

You may also take a ball of tin foil and poke the blade a few times into the cup, which will remove debris while also allowing a minor sharpening on them.

Blade

Cricut has a few different types of cutting blades and tips. Each blade has its own unique function enabling it to cut various materials.

Blade Housing

The blade housing is the cylindrical tube that holds the blade and fits into the blade head and blade accessory compartment of the Cricut cutting machine.

Blank

Cricut offers items, called blanks, to use with various projects for vinyl, iron-on, heat transfer vinyl, or infusible ink. These items include T-shirts, tote bags, coasters, and baby noisiest.

Brayer

The Brayer is a tool that looks a bit like a lint roller brush. It is used to flatten and stick material or objects down smoothly as it irons out bubbles, creases, etc.

Bright Pad

A Bright Pad is a device that looks like a tablet. This device has a strong backlight to light up materials to help with weeding and defining intricate cuts. It is a very handy tool to have and can be used for other DIY projects as well.

Butcher Paper

Butcher paper is the white paper that comes with the Cricut Infusible Inks sheets. It is used to act as a barrier between the EasyPress or iron when transferring the ink sheet onto a blank or item.

Carriage

The carriage is the bar in the Cricut cutting machine through which the blade moves.

Cartridge

Cartridges are what the older models of the Cricut cutting machine used to cut images. Each cartridge would hold a set of images. They can still be used with the Cricut Explore Air 2, which has a docking site for them. If you want to use them with a Cricut Maker, you will have to buy a USB adapter. Design Space still supports the use of Cartridge images.

Cartridges also come in a digital format.

Cricut Maker Adaptive Tool System

The Cricut Maker comes with an advanced tools system control using intricate brass gears. These new tools have been designed to aid the machine in making precise cuts and being able to cut more materials such as wood, metal, and leather.

Cut Lines

These are the lines along which the cutting machine will cut out the project's shapes.

Cutting Mat

There are a few different types of cutting mats also known as machine mats. Most of the large mats can be used on both the Cricut Explore Air 2 and the Cricut Maker. The Cricut Joy needs mats that are designed specifically for it.

Cut Screen

When you are creating projects in Design Space, there is a green button on the top right-hand corner of the screen called the Make it button. When the project is ready to be cut, this button is clicked on. Once that button has been clicked, the user is taken to another screen where they will see how the project is going to be cut out. This is the Cut Screen.

Drive Housing

The Drive Housing is different from Blade Housing in that it has a gold wheel at the top of the blade. These blades can only be used with the Cricut Maker cutting machine.

EasyPress

A Cricut EasyPress is a handheld pressing iron that is used for iron-on, heat transfer vinyl (HTV), and infusible ink. EasyPress's latest models are the EasyPress 2 and the EasyPress Mini.

EasyPress Mat

There are a few different EasyPress Mat sizes that are available on the market. These mats make transferring iron-on, heat transfer vinyl, and infusible ink a lot simpler. These mats should be used for these applications instead of an ironing board to ensure the project's success.

Firmware

Firmware is a software patch, update or newly added functionality for a device. For cutting machines, it would be new driver's updates, cutting functionality, and so on.

Both Design Space software on Cricut cutting machines and Cricut EasyPress 2 machines need to have their Firmware updated on a regular basis.

Go Button

This can also be called the "Cut" button. This is the button on the Cricut cutting or EasyPress machine that has the green Cricut "C" on it. It is the button that is pressed when a project is ready to be cut or pressed for the EasyPress models.

JPG File

A JPG file is a common form of digital image. These image files can be uploaded for use with a Design Space project.

Kiss Cut

When the cutting machine cuts through the material but not the material backing sheet, it is called a Kiss Cut.

Libraries

Libraries are lists of images, fonts, or projects that have been uploaded by the user or maintained by Cricut Design Space.

PNG File

A PNG file is another form of a graphics (image) file. It is most commonly used in Web-based graphics for line drawings, small graphic/icon images, and text.

Ready to Make Projects

Design Space contains ready-to-make projects that are projects that have already been designed. All the user has to do is choose the project to load in Design Space, get the material ready, and then make it to cut the design out. These projects can be customized as well.

Scraper Tool

The Scraper tool comes in small and large. It is used to make sure the material sticks firmly to a cutting mat, object, or transfer sheet.

Self-Healing Mat

Cricut has many handy accessories and tools to help with a person's crafting. One of these handy tools is the Self-Healing Mat. This mat is not for use in a cutting machine but can be used with handheld slicing tools to cut material to exact specifications

SVG File

The SVG file format is the most common format for graphic files in Cricut Design Space. This is because these files can be manipulated without losing their quality.

Transfer Sheet/Paper

A transfer sheet or transfer paper is a sheet that is usually clear and has a sticky side. These sheets are used to transfer various materials like transfer vinyl, sticker sheets, and so on to an item.

Weeding/Reverse Weeding

Weeding is the process of removing vinyl or material from a cut pattern or design that has been left behind after removing the excess material. For example, weeding the middle of the letter "O" to leave the middle of it hollow.

Reverse Weeding would be leaving the middle of the letter "O" behind and removing the outside of it.

Weeding Tool

The weeding tool has a small hooked head with a sharp point. This tool is used to pick off the material that is not needed on a cut. For instance, when cutting out the letter 'O,' the weeding tool is used to remove the middle of the letter so that it is hollow. Cleaning up a cut design with the Weeding tool is called weeding.

Conclusion

Congratulations on making it to the end. We hope that the chapters in this book have helped you get more familiar with your Cricut machine or that it has persuaded you to get one for the first time. There are so many amazing things that you can do with a Cricut machine. This book is only the beginning of what your creativity can get you if you work with the Cricut machine. There are only new and better updates that are happening to the machine, so now is the best time to get one and get in the door to understanding what it can do for you. We hope that the information we have provided you on what materials you can use with the machine, how to get your first project started, and all the project ideas are the tools you need to achieve the goals that you have with the Cricut machine.

The next step is to put what you have learned from this book into practice. Keep this book handy as you start out working with your Cricut machine so that you always have a quick reference guide with you. This is a great way for you to get to know the machine and not waste any time or material when you are just starting out. You can also remember that this book helps you through figuring out any problems you might face with the Design Space software or remembering any of the common mistakes that Cricut users can make with bad cuts. You should be well equipped to make all of the projects of your dreams and you are well on your way to impressing your friends and family with your newly acquired skill of homemade gifts and décor. You should also take the time to consider selling your projects to make a profit. You can have a really good side business in no time that can help you not only pay for the machine and the materials you are using, but also put some extra money in your pocket to pay your bills or get extra holiday gifts as well. There are many bonuses to getting a Cricut machine and we hope you have the opportunity to discover them all.

Happy crafting!

CRICUT DESIGN SPACE

MASTER THE USE OF YOUR CRICUT MACHINE TO MAKE AMAZING AND BEAUTIFUL CRAFTS AND PROJECTS AND AMAZE YOUR FAMILY AND FRIENDS

Samuel Blade

Introduction

Perhaps you've just purchased your first Cricut® or you've had one for some time but haven't tried it out yet, or you are fairly skilled but aren't sure how to use the Design Space.

This book will explain to you the whole thing you want to know about Cricut Design Space™.

Cricut has come a long way since it was first introduced in 2006 by Provo Craft & Novelty, Inc., and has undergone many changes. The corporation has released numerous versions of its die-cutting appliance as its fame among craftsperson has ascended. From its inception, the Cricut has provided many ways for a crafter to make beautiful things and sell them for a nice profit.

Most of us, whether we're Cricut pros or a beginner, have seen the many items for sale at craft shows and in specialty stores. Everything from popular saying and quotes stenciled on wood signs to monogrammed water tumblers and most everything in between.

Some Cricut users have mastered the machine and they can make vinyl letters look as if they were painted onto the wood. The vinyl meshes so well that with the naked eye you won't be able to find a spot to lift one of the vinyl letters. That's how realistic it can look. And, most types of vinyl are weather-resistant. That means you can make all kinds of awesome things for the outside as well as inside.

Cricut has come so far since the days of die-cutting for scrapbooking, and although scrapbooking is still popular, you don't see as many sheets of stickers in stores, and in some stores, the scrapbooking sector has shrunk since Cricut has become so much more than your scrapbooking partner.

And that's not to say scrapbooking isn't fun, but it is to say that ideas are endless and you can make almost anything you can think of.

Best of all, many Cricut models are Bluetooth enabled, making it easy to communicate with your other devices.

One of the nice features of a Cricut machine is that it doesn't take up too much space. It's about the size of a home printer; however, you will most likely want a large workspace for your tools and materials.

What Machine Should I Buy?

Before we get started on how to use the Design Space feature, let's evaluate the types of machines available. There are many to choose from and for first-time buyers, it can be daunting to select the right one. We'll focus on the more recent models. Your budget and how you intend to use the machine are big factors; however, you'll find most Cricut machines are around the same price with the exception of the Cuttlebug Machine.

This is a small, portable hand-crank machine that has a maximum cutting width of six inches. It only works with dies and embossing folders; however, it's perfect for those who are looking for a machine they can use for scrapbooking and card making.

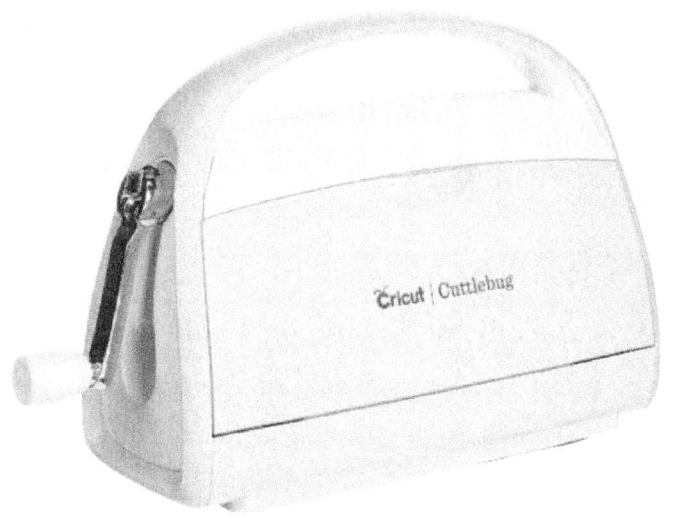

The hand-crank machine has been a staple in the Cricut family and you can usually find a new one for under $100. A used hand-crank can cost far less money. If it's in good condition and that's what you want, you can sometimes find them for as low as $25 at garage sales and garage sale sites.

This year, a new model was released called The Cricut Maker™. This has all the bells and whistles to do almost everything. It has the capability of cutting more materials than any preceding models and the company boasts its fast, precise cutting.

The Cricut Maker can be used with your own images, which is a plus for those who prefer to use their own or don't want to buy a subscription or pay for individual images. It allows you to personalize your items and make your own statement. You can make personalized cards, signs, and anything your heart desires. The ability to personalize your items with multiple lines and fonts broadens your horizon, and if you make products to sell, you can offer personalization.

The Cricut Maker is supposed to be better than the Cricut Explore Air 2 and is considered the top-of-the-line. The Explore is promoted as being easier to use than the Maker. It works with paper, vinyl, and cardstock, which is a plus.

Of course, you'll need the tools of the trade and these are sold in what are called "Bundles." There are many bundles available and you can purchase them alone or with your machine, with the exception of the hand-crank model.

A bundle includes the machine and a set of accessories. The bundles vary; however, many include printable sticker paper, cardstock, trimmers and cutting tools, pens, and usually free project ideas. Each model comes with a different bundle.

Once you have your machine, you'll need dies. There are two options: Cricut Access and Cricut Design Space.

The two are often confused, so let's touch briefly on the differences.

Cricut Access

When you purchased your Cricut, you may have been offered a 30-day free trial for Cricut Access.

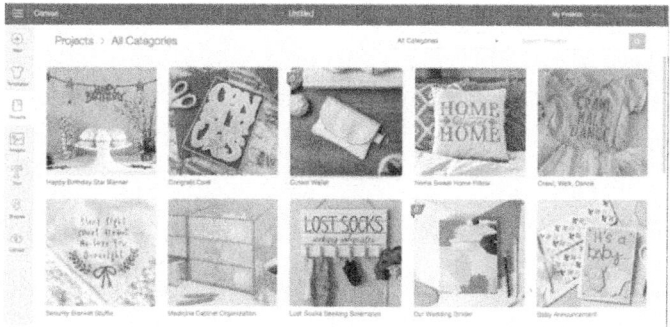

Cricut Access is a subscription-based program that gives you access to images and fonts without an extra charge, provided your subscription is up-to-date. The images and fonts are only available to those with an active subscription and if you don't pay, you'll no longer have access. The subscription is use-only; it does not allow you to keep the images and fonts. That is a common misconception.

How much you use your machine will determine if it's worth it for you to subscribe. If you're a heavy user and make a lot of different items, then a monthly or annual subscription might be right for you. This is a good choice if you're a crafter making a variety of items to sell.

Country stores and those selling folk art sometimes can't keep up with the demand for wooden or chalkboard signs. Sayings and inspirational quotes are popular right now, and if you're one of the lucky ones profiting from the craze, you'll get your money's worth from the subscription.

If you've decided that a subscription is a way to go, there are three options:

The monthly basic plan currently costs $9.99 per month and is billed monthly. The annual plan is $7.99 per month with a one-time annual billing of $95.88. The premium plan costs $119.88 annually.

Of course, you might be able to find a coupon code online and save a few dollars, and the premium subscription will give you 50% off on images and fonts not included in the basic subscription.

Cricut Access is used with Design Space.

Design Space

Cricut Design Space is an app that is used with the Cricut Explore and Cricut Maker™ machines. What makes Design Space unique is that it lets you wirelessly cut your designs.

You can get Cricut Design Space from the Apple™ store as a free download.

The app offers you access to Make It Now™ projects and fonts in the Cricut® Image Library along with thousands of images, according to Apple's promo.

Apple describes Cricut Design Space as an app offering the following features:

- Design and cut DIY projects with Cricut Explore and Cricut Maker cutting machines
- Choose from over 50,000 images, fonts, and projects in the Cricut Image Library—or use your own images and fonts for free
- Upload and clean up your own images
- Design and cut without an Internet connection using fonts and images downloaded to your device
- Cut quick and easy predesigned Make It Now™ projects

- Use the fixed camera on your device to position and visualize your projects on a real-life background
- Create party and home decorations, scrapbooking, cards, invitations, fashion, jewelry, kids' artistries, and others
- Cut an extensive diversity of materials together with vinyl, paper, cardstock, poster board, iron-on, fabric—even thicker supplies such as leather
- Sign in with your Cricut ID to access your images and projects and for easy checkout when making purchases on Cricut.com or in Design Space
- Bluetooth® wireless capability. By now, you've probably downloaded an app from the Apple Store, so we'll bypass instructions as to how to do so. If you've never done it before, use the Apple Store help menu and it'll be self-explanatory.

With these explanations behind us, let's begin taking the steps you'll need to successfully use Cricut Design Space.

Now that we've been introduced, let's get started!

Chapter 1: Introduction to Cricut Design Space

The Design Space Application

The Cricut Design Space Application is one that is run entirely from your browser. This means that you will need an active internet connection so as to use it, but downloading that plugin will allow you to leap in and out of the Cricut Design Space as you wish from your device. This plugin will allow you to log in from your computer and your login information will allow you to download the plugin on any device you select so that you can move from computer to computer with ease!

Upon your first login to the Cricut Design Space, you will be prompted to tell the program the type of Cricut machine that you'd wish to install. This may tell the program what type of machine it will be communicating with so it can make sure that it's properly laying out all of your cuts, lines, and scores. Once you have completed this step and your computer has properly identified your device, you can click the "New Project" button that is situated in the upper right-hand corner. This is often where you will be prompted to download the installer for the Cricut Design

Space plugin that will allow your computer and Cricut Design Space to attach with each other.

Opening the Cricut Design Space Plugin Installer for the first time will prompt you to link your device to the Cricut machine that you have selected. Establishing this connection will allow your computer to communicate seamlessly with your Cricut machine. Once the connection is established between your computer and your machine, you will be able to create projects whenever you'd like without having to reestablish that connection. This means that you can import images from other sources, images that you have created by yourself, or you can use any of the various images that Cricut offers either for free through Cricut Design Space or through their paid Access subscription.

The first thing you ought to know about Cricut Access is that it is not required that you have this subscription to use Cricut Design Space. You can make use of Cricut Design Space and each feature that it has to give without fear of being stuck behind a paywall.

The benefits that a crafter gets from signing up for a Cricut Access membership will vary depending on the subscription tier that you have chosen. At this point, there are three subscription tiers available through the Cricut Access program.

These member perks can make all the difference for the crafter that's avidly creating many projects in a short period of time. Again, these subscriptions are in no way compulsory for crafters who wish to make use of the Cricut Design Space or its user-friendly interface, but these substantial benefits are what you can expect from the membership if you choose to sign up!

Your First Design

The first thing that will be presented to you when you launch Cricut Design Space for the first time is a quick tutorial on how to insert a shape into the Cricut Design Space, also on how to fill that inserted shape with a colored pattern. You may want to offer that process a couple of trial runs until you are perfectly conversant in all the steps and various assets and options. You will be able to introduce a shape into Cricut Design Space, change its Linetype, and alter what the space is crammed with. Once you have mastered that, you can have quite a head start on deciding the way to do more projects in the Cricut Design Space.

Now that you have gotten a bit of an introduction to the fundamentals of Cricut Design Space, let's run through a fast project to get you conversant in the whole process.

Initially, you will need to select the "Text" option. In the text box that appears, you are going to type the phrase "Good Vibes," and pick a font that's available in the Cricut Design Space that you like for this project. Please keep in mind that a number of the fonts that are available in Cricut Design Space come with a price. If you are looking to find only fonts that are free, you can choose the "System Fonts," which limits you to only the fonts that are already installed on your computer. The positive thing here is that you can find fonts from other sources and use them to fit your specific needs.

Once you have chosen a font that is right for you and your project, make sure that the "Linetype" is about to "cut." Once you have checked this and made sure that the settings are appropriate, you can then click "Make it," in the upper right-hand corner of your screen and follow the prompts that come in front of the screen. If the design seems like it is properly placed on the screen that pops up following this step, then you can continue to the subsequent steps.

You will notice that, at the top of the screen, there are helpful little measurements. Using those measurements, you can cut a bit of self-adhesive vinyl that is sized appropriately to accommodate the design you have created. Using your light blue or light grip Cricut Maker mat, you can set up your vinyl, so it lines up with the design on your screen. Your designs are going to be cut directly from the piece you are layering onto the mat. If you want to make adjustments to your design, now is the right time to do so!

Once your vinyl is where you want it to be and your design has been adjusted to your specification, you can use the scraper/burnishing tool to smooth your vinyl down onto the gripped surface of your mat. Using the back of the tool will help it to glide more smoothly without leaving any scratches on your vinyl. You will need to smooth it down from the center, working outward toward the sides. Make sure that your piece is lying completely flat with no folds, bubbles, or imperfections made along the way. This may offer you the sharpest, cleanest, crispest cuts possible.

Now that your vinyl has been properly burnished onto the mat and you are ready to advance, you will need to set your Cricut machine to the "vinyl" setting so your machine applies the blade to the material with the acceptable pressure for your material. You can skip this step if you have a Cricut Maker, as that model will do that part automatically. Slide your mat under the mat guides in your Cricut machine. Once you have done that, you'll click "Continue" on the bottom right of Cricut Design Space and the site will begin to communicate with your machine. Once it is in the right place, push the mat toward the rollers and click on the flashing Load/Unload button that's marked with a double arrow.

This may load the mat into the machine and lock it into place so your cuts are more precise.

Once the Cricut C button begins to flash, you ought to press it once and watch your Cricut machine go to work. Once the machine has completed its cut, remove the mat from the machine and bring it into your crafting space. Using the rounded back of your scraper/burnishing tool, you will need to smooth down the whole surface of the vinyl on your mat. This may help the design to release more independently from the mat while you are weeding.

Once the vinyl has been thoroughly burnished, you can use the weeding tool to select up the blanks in the center and surrounding the letters in your design. Once you have done this, you will find that each one that's left on the carrier sheet is your design. This is often when you will layer your transfer tape onto your design and burnish it completely. Once it is fully burnished with your scraper/burnishing tool, you will want to use lotion to cleanse the surface that you wish to emblazon your design. I chose the back of my laptop.

Line up the transfer tape and your design up with the surface onto which you plan to place your design. Lay the design down and, using the scraper/burnishing tool, calculate all the bubbles and imperfections until the design is clinging completely flat and comfortable to the surface that you have chosen. Now, using the skinny side of your scraper/burnishing tool, pull up one corner of the transfer tape and slowly roll the tape back until it's lifted completely off of the surface and your design, taking care to press the letters down in any places where they could try to come up along the way.

Once your transfer tape has come far away from your surface, you ought to be left to admire your very first Cricut project! Great work!

Working with Cricut Design Space Layers Panel

Space design is a very complex tool you can use on your desktop, laptop, tablet, or smartphone; you can help make the most amazing projects with your Cricut machine. You can cut, print, punctuate, or write; you can adjust the dimensions or other image parameters, add new items (such as images, projects, sources), help customize their projects, and much more. Space design can do a lot for you, and that is why you need to know your panels or windows correctly. Perhaps the most important thing is the panel layers and seeing the canvas, but I will not spoil it for you. However, you need to read the following for a far better understanding of those windows.

Chapter 2: Open an Account

Cricut Design Space is a web-based program used by Cricut machine for creating, browsing predesigned projects/images and editing projects before cutting. You can make use of any compatible internet-enabled devices including desktop, tablet, phone or laptop.

The program was designed by Provo Craft to be user-friendly. However, the level of simplicity depends on your general knowledge of computers. If you are tech-savvy, then perhaps you can navigate design space...with some effort. Otherwise, you will definitely require some help.

There are over 50,000 images that you can choose from in the library of Cricut Design Space, coupled with the 800+ predesigned projects will ensure you never run out of design ideas.

The other fantastic and amazing feature of the Cricut Design Space is the ability to upload your own predesigned images and fonts to be used for the project you intend to execute.

The formats of the images used by Design Space software are the jpg, bmp, gif, png, svg, and dxf files.

You have the ability to assess the program from multiple computers and mobile devices. This is because the Cricut Design Space is a cloud-based program. This gives you the freedom to work from anywhere and everywhere there is an internet connection. You can also start and end on a different device as long as they are all connected to the internet.

Note that Cricut Design Space is not compatible with some devices including computers running Unix/Linux OS and Chromebooks.

There are many tools, buttons, options that are displayed on the Canvas that makes the Cricut Design Space look difficult for first-time users. However, after reading through this guide book, you will not only be a master of the Cricut Design Space, but you will also obtain good value for the money spent. It is important to state here that definitions and terms used were taken from the original manufacturer of the machine as described in www.cricut.com.

Compatibility

It is practically impossible to develop any program that is compatible with every device on the planet. If there are programs like that, I do not know but what I do know is that every program has compatibility requirements and the Cricut Design Space program is no exception.

There are minimum requirements for different platforms to enable efficient use of the Design Space for Cricut Machine as described in System Requirement below.

System Requirement

The minimum system requirement for Design Space software for Windows OS includes:

- Windows 8 or later;
- 4Gb RAM size;
- 50MB free disk space;
- Available USB port or Bluetooth enabled;
- Minimum display screen resolution of 1024px X 768px.

The minimum requirement for Mac OS includes:

- Mac OS X10.12 or later;
- 183GHz CPU;
- 4GB RAM size;
- 50MB free disk space;
- The USB port, Bluetooth connection, and screen display resolution remain the same as that of Windows.

- 2–3Mbps Download and 1–2Mbps Upload is required for internet connection.

For Android devices, the minimum OS requirement is Android 6.0 or higher in order to work perfectly, but there are factors that also determine the performance of this device. These factors are the manufacturer, chipset, and the speed of the device.

Other compatible devices include Galaxy S, Galaxy Note, Galaxy Tab A, Galaxy Tab S series; these LG series: G, K, or V; and for Motorola: Droid G, Z, E, Turbo or Moto series.

Online/Offline

One notable feature with the iOS devices, as stated above, is their ability to work in offline mode (without an internet connection) as well as in online mode. Secondly, the memory usage varies as the device usage while working offline.

To work in online mode is simpler compared to offline mode. All you need to do is to connect to the internet with your device and log in to your Cricut account. Of course, you can do more with the online mode than with the offline mode.

To work in offline mode, you will need to download the content onto your device. The downloaded content will be used by Cricut Design Space to design and cut materials without connection to the internet. Isn't this wonderful? Yes, it is, but this feature is limited to only iOS devices.

Subscription

Cricut has a library with tens of thousands of images that have been optimized to cut with speed and accuracy. There are three sources of an image in the Cricut library that are identified as Cricut images, Designer images, and Licensed images.

Cricut images are the original images developed by the Cricut crew, Designer images are images developed in partnership with top designers, and Licensed images are designs and characters from partner brands like Marvel, Disney, and Hello Kitty.

The visualization of these images is free, but you will require a subscription when you need to use them for projects that arise. This is an amazing marketing strategy to help their clients know the suitability of such images for their projects before purchasing them.

Cricut Access is the medium used for the subscription. It gives you access to the Cricut library with over 50,000 images, 370+ fonts, and over 1000 predesigned projects at no additional cost to you.

All images, fonts, cartridges, and projects included in your membership of Cricut Access are denoted by a little green flag that permits ease of search for Cricut Access images.

Another benefit of subscription is that the member is granted 10% off orders in Cricut Design Space and on cricut.com. Another amazing marketing strategy by Cricut.

The subscription to Cricut Access is $95.80 per year and $9.99 for a monthly subscription. The choice is therefore yours to make in order to have access to the benefits stated above. Do not let this be a limitation to the use of your Cricut Design Space or having unlimited access to images in the Cricut library.

Chapter 3: Downloading and Installing Design Space

After setting up your Cricut machine according to the instruction, there will be directions on your screen that you must follow to create your first project. You will still be using the link you found on the paper when you were setting up your machine. If you have not received your machine yet and are interested in knowing how it works, or you are looking for extra clarifications, here's what it will tell you.

First Step

First off, load a pen into the accessories clamp. You can pick whichever color you think will go best with the paper you have received. Next, you want to turn the knob so that the indicator is pointed to "cardstock," considering that is what you will be working with. Have you already had a proper look at your mats? The blue mat is what you will want to use for this project. You should remove the plastic cover—keep it, don't throw it away as you will need to recover your mat when you're done to avoid dust accumulation—and lay down the paper on the mat with the top left corners of the material and the grid aligned.

Second Step

Make sure that the paper is pressed flat before you push it between the rollers firmly. The mat has to rest on the bottom roller. When it is in place, press the "Load" button to load your mat between the rollers. Press the "go" button, which will be flashing at this stage, and wait for the machine to work its magic on your project. Once everything is done, the light will flash, and you can press the "Load" button again to unload the mat. Your paper will still be sticking to the mat when you remove it.

Third Step

Be careful when removing the material from the mat. Don't be too hasty; take your time so that it doesn't tear. Pull the mat away from the cardstock instead of doing it the other way around. After completing that step, you can now fold the cardstock in half, insert the liners into the corner slots of the card, and it's done!

You have just made your first Cricut project in a matter of minutes from start to finish! Congratulations! What are you waiting for? Do more projects! There are a ton of templates you can play around with—practice, practice, practice.

Launching the Platform Downloading and Installing, Cricut Access

Unlimited Access to more than 400 attractive fonts.

Unlimited Access to more than 50,000 cut-ready, covet-worthy premium Cricut images.

10% discounts on every product you purchase on cricut.com. This includes machines, materials, accessories, and many more (including sale items).

10% discounts on Premium licensed images, fonts, and ready-to-make projects. These projects are from brands such as Disney, Anna Griffin, and Simplicity.

Priority member care line (50% reduction in wait time).

Downloading Cricut Design Space

The first stage of learning the Cricut Design Space is to know how to download and install it correctly. The steps are not so complicated, all you need is to have the basic computer skills, i.e., know your way around your PC or Desktop. Follow the steps below to get your Design Space downloaded, installed, and launched.

Go to your internet browser on your PC or Desktop, then open the following address to access the Cricut design website.

Once you are on the platform, select "Download." The download should start immediately, and the display will change once it starts downloading. However, the display could be quite different depending on the browser you are using. The screenshots being used are from Google Chrome.

Installing Cricut Design Space

Once the download has been completed, either go to your "Downloads" folder or double-click on the file that appears after the download on your browser.

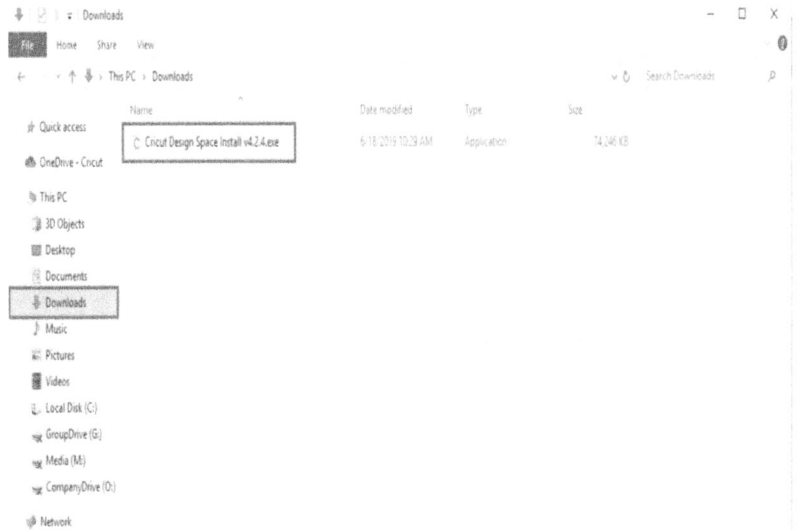

You might get a popup, asking you if you want to trust the application or not, select "Yes" and wait for the next window.

You should have a setup window displaying the installation progress popup shortly after.

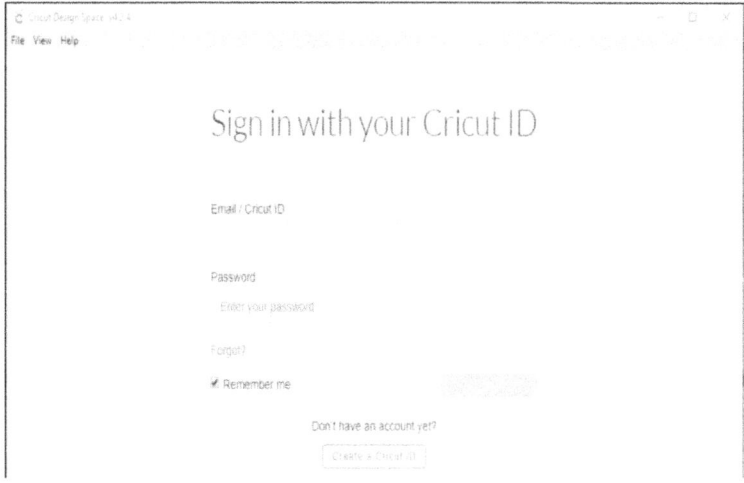

Go ahead and input your registered ID and password on Cricut to sign in.

For most computers, a Design Space icon gets added automatically to your home screen. Right-click the icon and then select "Pin to Taskbar," or get the icon dragged to the taskbar to get the shortcut pinned for easy access.

And that's it! You're done with the installation of your Design Space. That wasn't so hard, was it? You can now proceed to launch the app when you are ready. You can also share your feedback by using the feedback tab located at the lower part of the design space menu.

Lastly, you need to ensure that your Design Space has the latest version. This will make sure you're up to date with all that Cricut offers and you get the best results from your Cricut machine. To find the current version of your Design Space application, follow the steps below:

- Left-click on the small arrow located on the Taskbar to reveal hidden icons.
- Place your mouse on top of the Design Space icon (don't click).
- The Cricut Bridge version should appear.

Chapter 4: Canvas

Design Space Canvas (Design Panel, Header, Zoom)

Think of the "Design Space" canvas as your playground where you can turn your ideas into reality. You'll be able to create new projects, add images or texts to your existing projects and continue editing them until you're happy with the results. So, here is an overview of different elements of the "Design Space" canvas, as shown in the picture below:

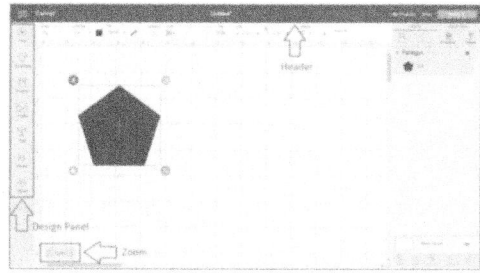

Design Panel

- **New**—To start building a new project you must always click on the "New" tab.

- **Templates**—To view your final design in real life background, you can use any of the relevant templates by clicking on the "Templates" tab.
- **Projects**—To search, select, and cut designs from an already existing project, you can use the "Projects" tab, which will contain a variety of other projects along with your own projects.
- **Images**—The "Cricut Image Library" contains a wide variety of pictures available at your fingertips for free and to buy. The "Images" tab will also contain any image that you may upload. So, you can click on the images icon to search, select, and insert any desired image into the Canvas.
- **Text**—You can use the "Text" tab to add desired phrases or words directly to the Canvas.
- **Shape**—You can use the "Shape" tab to insert simple shapes square, rectangle, triangle, circle, and score lines into your Canvas.
- **Upload**—You can use the "Upload" tab to use your own image files including the most commonly used file types at no charge.

Header

- **Menu**—The "hamburger" icon on the top left of the screen will allow you to navigate through "Cricut Design Space." You can directly access "Home," "Canvas," and several other "Design Space" features, such as "Settings," "New Machine Setup," "Help," "Link Cartridges," and "Sign Out."
- **Page Title**—This will help you remember whether you're on the "Home" or "Canvas" page of the "Design Space." By clicking on the "Page Title," you'll be able to close an open tab.
- **Project Name**—This will show you the name of your project. If you've not already saved your project, then "Untitled" will be displayed as the name of the project.
- **My Projects**—You can open your saved projects by clicking on "My Projects."
- **Save**—In order to access your projects across your devices and multiple platforms, you must save your projects to your account by clicking on the "Save" icon and providing a name for your projects. Note: If you'd like to keep your project private and all to yourself, then make sure you uncheck the "Public" option while saving your project. Once the project has been saved and you'd like to rename

your project, just click on "Save As" and enter a new name for your project.

- **Make it**—Click on the "Make It" icon when you've prepped your mats and are ready to transfer your project to your "Cricut" machine.

Zoom

- You can "Zoom In" to look at the finer details of your project and "Zoom Out" to see an overview of the same.

Setting Up Your Cricut Machine on Canvas

To get started with your projects, you must first set up your cutting machine on the "Design Space" using your "Cricut ID" by following the instructions below:

1. Click on the hamburger icon next to the "Canvas" on the top left of the screen.
2. Click on "New Machine Setup" from the available options.
3. You'll see the different "Cricut" devices on your screen. Simply select the device you're looking to pair.

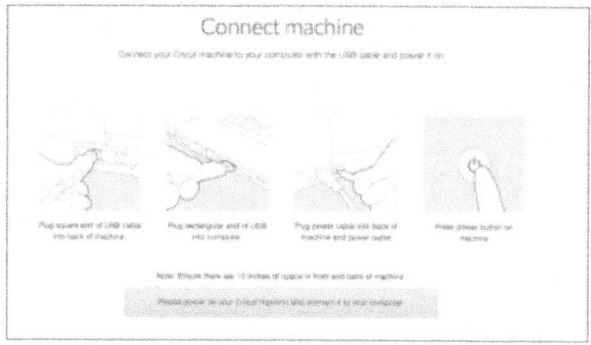

4. Follow the instructions on the screen, as shown in the picture below.
5. Click "Continue" and you're all set!
6. Note: If you've another device that you've just purchased and need to set up. Follow the instructions above and simply select the other device that you need to set.

Design Space Environment

You need to learn more about Design Space before you start with your first Cricut projects for beginners. Before we dive into the magnificent world of Cricut designs and crafting projects made with Cricut, we need to address the very core of designing projects—Cricut machine software known as Design Space. Here is everything you need to know about Design Space before you can start using Cricut for your projects.

How to Use Design Space Canvas?

We will get into the details on how to work in Canvas and how to insert your images and patterns, edit your designs and perform other actions that can be done in Design Space. Let's see how you can start working in Canvas, step by step.

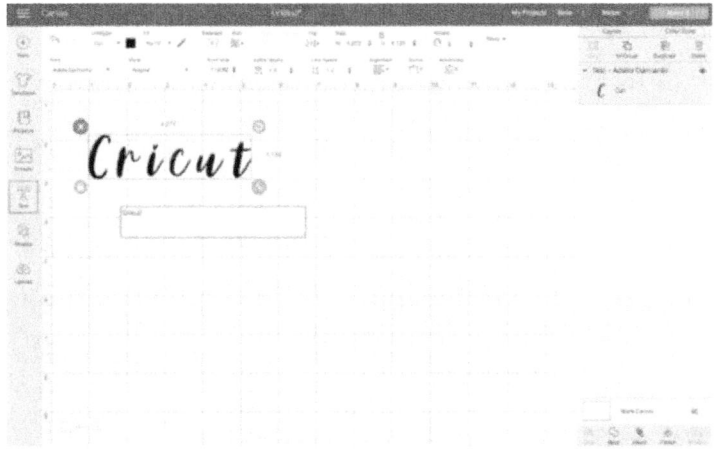

This is how the Canvas window looks like when active, while you can also notice that you have numerous options and commands within the software.

Canvas Editing Area

Canvas editing area is the segment where you'll do all your edits, which includes arranging project elements in the canvas area and editing your designs. The editing area is located on the top of the Canvas and also allows changing fonts, size of fonts, and designs, as well as enables alignment of design pieces. This is where you're preparing your project from scratch. The editing of area/panel can be divided into two subareas or subpanels. The top panel of the Canvas editing area serves the purpose of holding the main functions for creating new projects, save your projects once your design is ready and send your designs to the machine to start making projects. The second sub-panel found at the bottom of the Canvas editing panel holds commands for designing and editing your projects.

Top Editing Subpanel

The top editing subpanel is comprised of several important functions. If you click on "Canvas," you'll gain access to the Toggle menu—more details on what you can do with the Toggle menu will be disclosed further. You can also see the next command shown as "Untitled"—this is where you name your projects, following the list of your saved projects under "My project," "Save" button, and "Maker" (Machine button) and the execution button "Make it" colored in green.

Home

Canvas

New Machine Setup
Calibration
Manage Custom Materials
Update Firmware
Account Details
Link Cartridges
Cricut Access
Settings
Legal
New Features
United States ▼
Help
Sign Out

Canvas—Toggle Menu

Although you can gain access to the Toggle menu through the "Canvas" menu and Canvas window, the Toggle menu is not directly related to editing functions and commands crucial for working in the editing area of Canvas. Still, it would be handy for you to find your way around the Toggle menu, which is why we're also addressing these commands. You'll find all commands regarding the software right here in this dropping menu. You can view your profile from the Toggle menu, update your firmware and software, perform setup for your new machine, check your account details, link cartridges, manage your subscription through Cricut Access, access settings, features, and find the Help button for support from Cricut. You can also sign out from your account through the Toggle menu. The settings option will allow adjusting the visibility and measurements for your Canvas area.

Project Name (Untitled*)

All new projects start with "Untitled" tags, while this is the area where you can name your projects that can be later viewed and accessed under the "My projects" sector. You won't be able to name your project until you start working in the sense of adding at least one element to the Canvas area.

My Projects

Every project you save and name can be found under "My projects," you can save as many projects as you like and reuse them by redesigning, re-cutting, and editing. This is where you'll find an entire list of all the saved projects, which is handy since you might want to work on a project similar to what you've already done. That way, you don't always need to start from scratch.

Save Button

Save option won't be available until you start working in the Canvas area and have at least placed one element or pattern on the Canvas. Once you start working, the Save button will become active and you can click on it to save your projects. All projects are saved on the Cricut cloud storage space, while you can also save your project as you're working on it to prevent losing your work in case of a potential crash of the cloud system. This is less likely to happen, but if you want to be on the safe side, you can save your project as you're working on it, saving your project every time you make some progress.

Maker (Machine)

You can click on this button to access your machine options. This button represents your Cricut machine, and depending on which machine you've used for crafting, you'll have different options available.

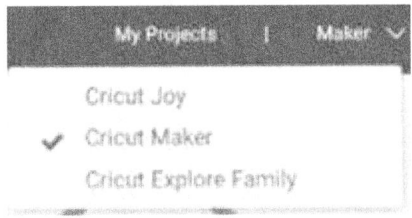

Once you click on the Maker option, (machine), you'll access all your machines that have been already set up in case you're using more than one Cricut model. Model Maker has different options than other machines.

Make It Button

Once you've finished with editing and designing, you can save your project in case you wish to keep it in the library "My projects," then click on the "Make it" button to prepare for cutting. You can prepare several mats at a time, preparing more cuts and placing them in the queue. You can choose which design should be cut first as you'll have all your prepared mats categorized by color on the left side of the window.

Bottom Editing Subpanel

The second subpanel of the editing menu has multiple controls for designing and editing your projects. In case you've already worked with software such as Illustrator, Photoshop, or similar software, you'll find most commands familiar. Even if you've never worked on similar software, you'll find most of the commands and options to be logical and self-explanatory.

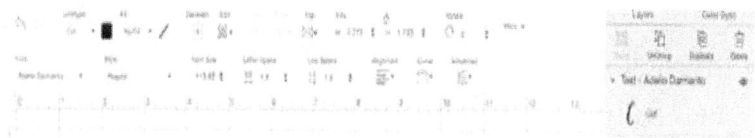

Nevertheless, to help you find your way around the editing panel, we will go through each command available in the second subpanel. You'll use these functions to edit your materials and create your designs.

Undo/Redo

This is probably a familiar function, as you can use these buttons (arrows) to correct your mistakes and get back to the earlier version of your design with one click. Making mistakes and changing your mind on shapes and colors is a natural thing during the creative process, which is how these buttons become more than handy.

Linotype

Linotype and fill are options related to the type of blade you wish to use on a given project. Depending on which Cricut machine model you're using, you'll have different options for cutting. Once you choose the machine you want to cut with, you'll be presented with different types of blades and cutting available for that machine. Based on which material you're using for your project; you can choose the type of blade. As far as options for cutting style are concerned, you've more than several options to choose from—Wave, Perforation, Deboss, Score, Engrave, Cut, and Draw. All these options are available with Cricut Maker. In case you're using other machines, there'll be fewer options to choose from, making the cutting styles more basic when compared to options available with Maker.

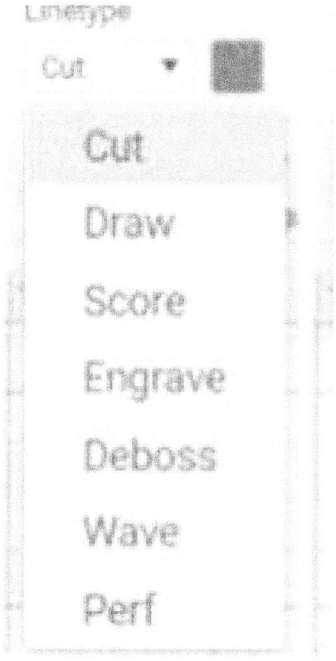

This is how the drop-down menu will look like if you're using Maker once you click on the Linetype option.

As you may notice, in case you're using Explore instead of Maker, there'll be only three options to choose from.

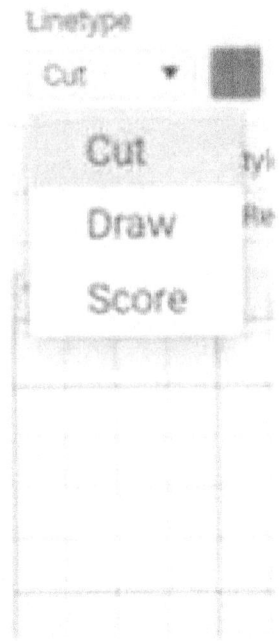

The "Cut" option will be your default line type until you've uploaded your design file, which is when you can choose other options as well. The machine won't cut your design until you choose the "Make it" command.

Chapter 5: Canvas Tips and Tricks

A lot of people have issues with printing and cutting a design. Let's assume you have a design of a puppy. To print and cut this design follow the next steps:

- Make sure your printer is connected to your pc.
- First, send your design to print on your printer.
- Take the printed-out design and load it on a cutting mat on your Cricut.
- Hit Make It on the top right Conner in Design Space.
- Design space would then guide you through the simple cutting process, prompting you to print and then cut.
- To get a single printable image, select all the individual layers on your layer panel and click on flatten. This would ensure that when cutting, Cricut makes a cut over the entire design as a single unit instead of cutting all the individual layers.
- There is a good number of ready-to-make projects in the Design Space. However, you may want to make a few changes to some of these projects before you print/cut. To

do this, all you need to do is click on your desired ready-to-make project. Once it opens, look at the top right corner of the screen (beside the make It command), if the design is customizable, Design Space will open the design in the canvas area for you to make the modifications you desire. You can change text; delete elements you don't need or add up elements to your taste to customize the ready-to-make projects.

- To reduce the size of an image in Design Space you can use the handle at the bottom-right edge of the image when selected. Alternatively, use the "size" tool in the top panel to set the exact size you want.

- Use the "cut" linetype option for the design you want to cut alone. On the other hand, if you want to cut and print a design, select the print option as the linetype.

- Design Space can be used both on your desktop and on your mobile device. However, if you are a beginner, I would advise you to use your desktop to learn as it provides better viewing and enhanced user experience. With time, your confidence level will increase and you'll become more comfortable designing on your phone. Design Space comes with all these many tools that may come off as overwhelming to the beginner. Using a laptop or desktop would greatly increase the rate at which you learn.

- To select multiple layers, click on one layer and hold cmd or ctrl key, then continue clicking on all the other layers you wish to select. You'll know a layer has been selected when it's highlighted in blue.
- To edit a text, double-click on the text on your canvas.
- To duplicate a shape, right-click on the shape and select "duplicate" from the drop-down menu.

Basic Design Space Keyboard Shortcuts

- To delete an element on your canvas, simply click on the element and hit the delete key on your keyboard.
- To copy an element, hit ctrl/cmd C on your keyboard.
- To paste an element, click on the element and hit ctrl/cmd V on your keyboard.
- To cut an object, select the object and hit ctrl/cmd X on your keyboard.
- Copying and pasting an element creates a second copy/duplicates the element.
- To select all the elements on your canvas, hit ctrl/cmd A on your keyboard.
- To save your project, hit ctrl/cmd S.
- To remove the gridlines from the canvas, hit on ctrl/cmd on your keyboard.

Chapter 6: How to Use Design Space

Guidelines on Editing Layers in Cricut Design Space

There is no way that your creative juices won't flow with the several layers of SVG files offered by Cricut. Obey the instructions below to edit SVG files' layers in the Cricut Design Space without a hassle:

Uploading the SVG

The first step in editing the SVG is to upload it. Then, the layers will be displayed on the toolbar on the right. The method employed in creating a design will dictate the number of layers an SVG will have; more complicated designs have more layers. The complexity of the design will force you to get more intuitive. The toolbar has some great functions that let the user edit the layers:

Layer editing: Slice, Attach, Contour, Weld, Flatten, Group, Ungroup, Duplicate, Delete.

Color synchronization: this option leaves room for selecting two or more layers and then synchronizing the colors.

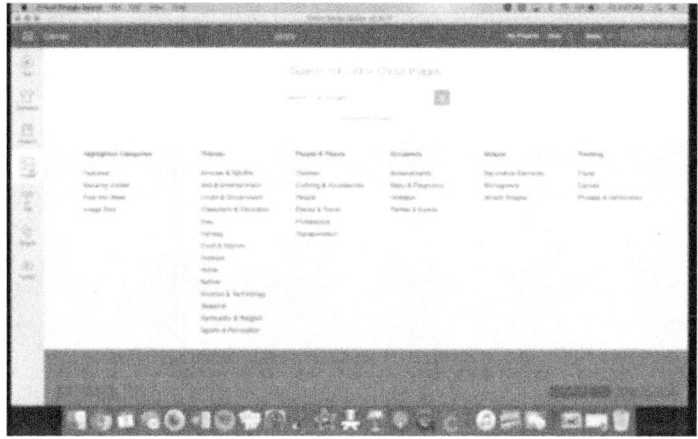

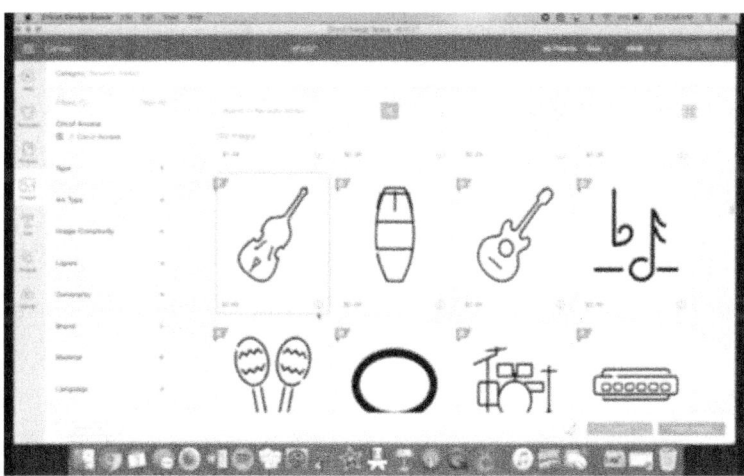

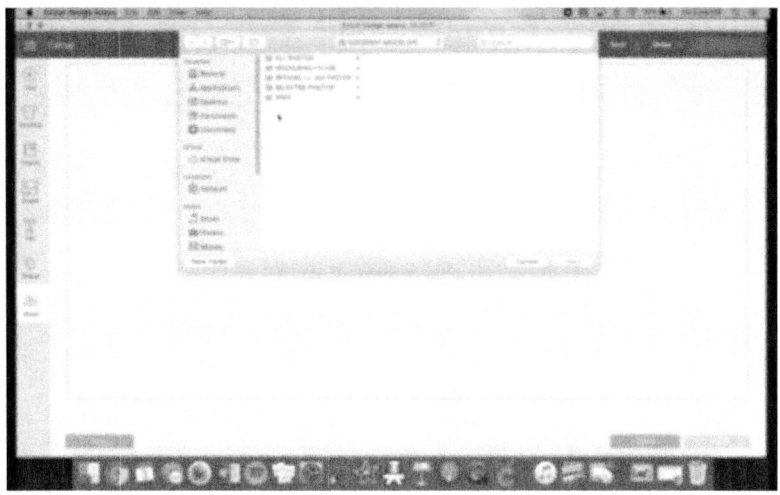

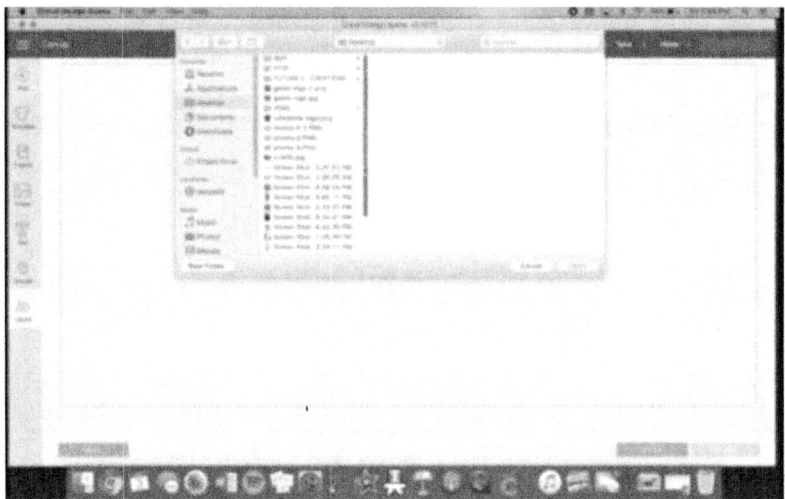

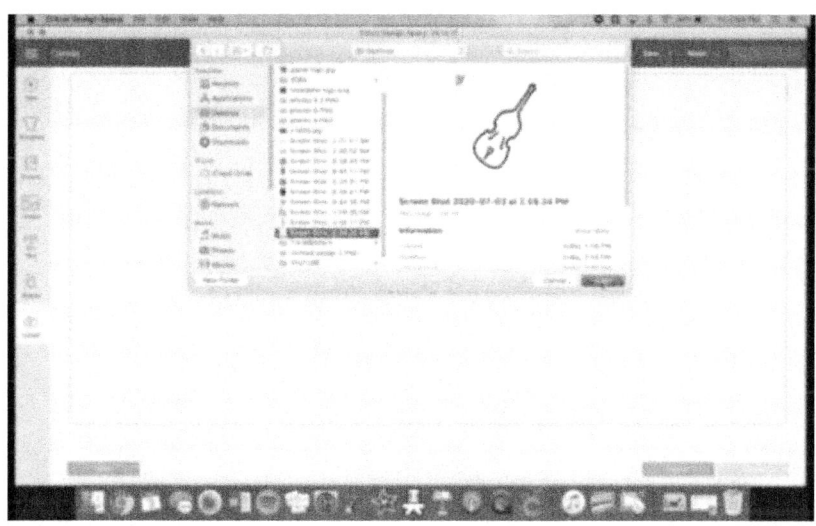

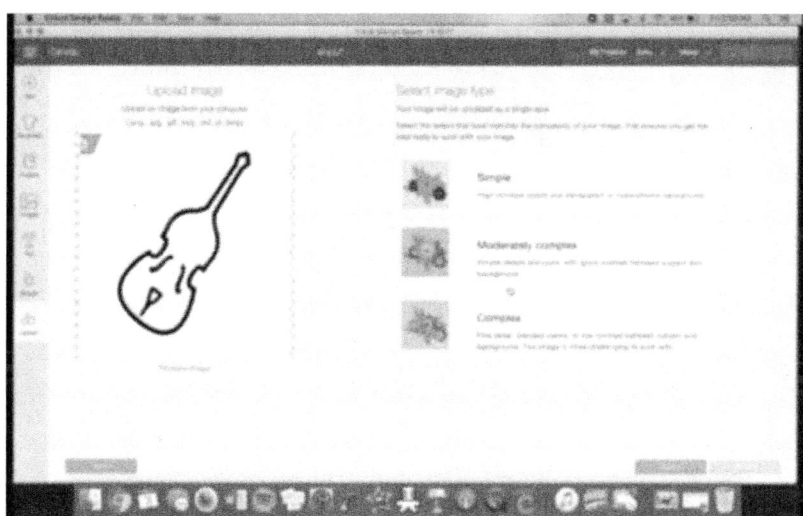

163

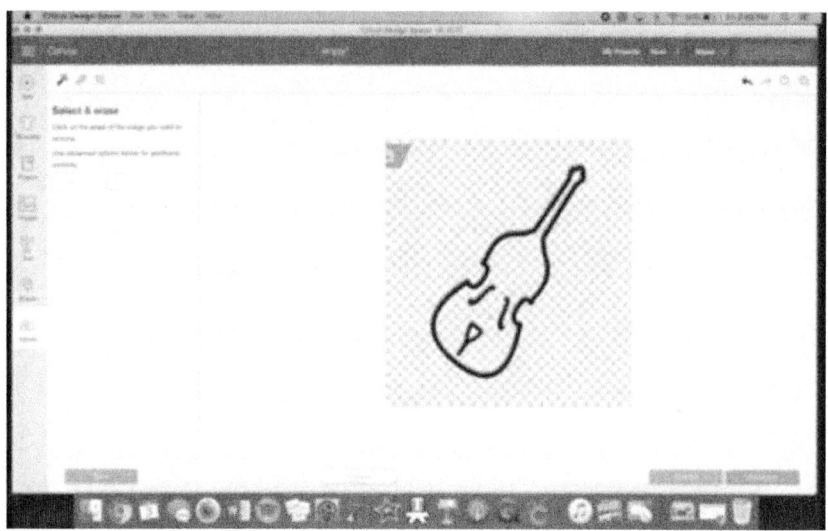

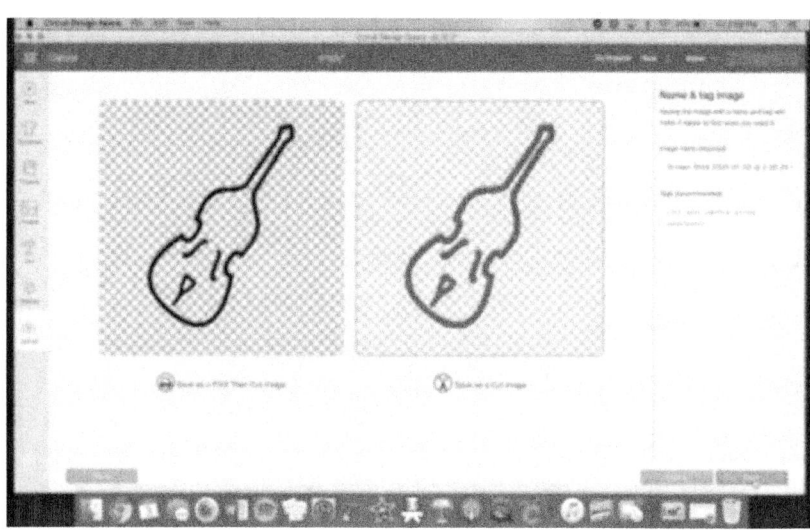

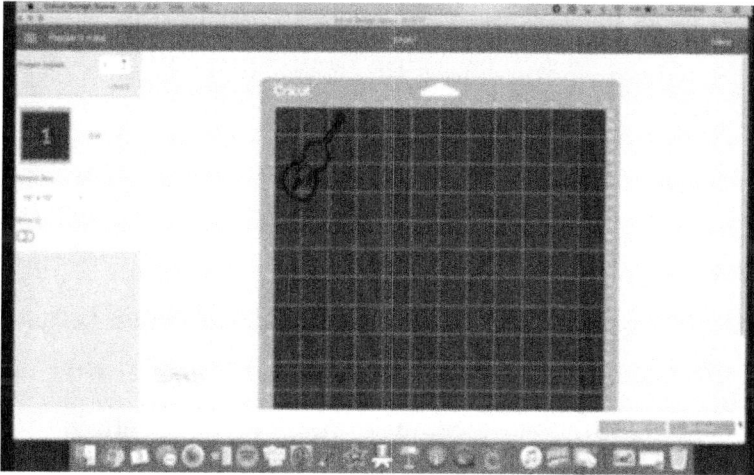

Editing an SVG

The first step in editing an SVG file is to ungroup the file. Ungrouping is done by highlighting the file and then clicking on "Ungroup" in the toolbar on the right; this will split the SVG into several layers. It doesn't take much to group the layers to how they were; all you need to do is select the layers and click "Group" on the toolbar on the canvas area. This will also help you to modify every layer at once. A click on the eye near the layers will conceal a layer.

Editing the SVG Colors

The color modification of an SVG can have a significant impact on the design's outlook. There are two ways to modify the layers' color:

- Synchronize the colors of several layers
- Alter the colors of the layers separately

Synchronizing the colors of several layers is time and material saving because it is sure that the layers will take on the same colors in print. The first step in synchronizing colors is to add the colors you need. For example, if you need to use purple, orange, and blue, open the "Color Sync" in the toolbar and then drag and drop the shape on the color you want the layer to be.

Modifying the colors of layers separately can be achieved without stress by the toolbar on the right. You just have to highlight the layer you wish to modify and alter the color in "Materials color" at the toolbar on the right.

Taking a Layer Out

There are two methods of removing a layer from an assignment: select the layer and eliminate it using the "Delete" tool on the toolbar on the right, or selecting the layer and then clicking the "red x" at the edge of the highlighted square.

Organizing and Bringing Layers into Line

There are options in the Cricut Design Space's toolbar that can help to reorganize and bring the layers that are not well arranged in a line. The options include:

- **Aligning layers:** after highlighting the layers, you want to bring into a line, click on "Align" in the upper toolbar. This click will reveal another set of the menu on how to align the layers.
- **Organize layers:** the upper toolbars do a great job of organizing the SVG layers. To organize layers, highlight the layers first and click on "Arrange" in the upper toolbar. The click will introduce another set of options that are explained below:
    - **Move Forward:** this function will transfer the highlighted item a step forward in the stacking order, making the item be one layer above the Layers Panel.

- o **Send to front:** this tool will transfer the highlighted item a step in front of the stacking order, making the item be one layer at the upper part of the Layers Panel.
- o **Send to back:** this option transfers the highlighted item behind the stacking order, thus displaying the item at the Layers panel base.

Flattening the Layers

Flattening fuses highlighted layers of a complete creation that are ready for printing. To highlight the layers, click on "Flattened," and the layers will be joined as one. You can then print your project.

Welding the Layers

Welding joins two layers to make one item. To weld, highlight the layers you desire to merge, and then click on "Weld" in the right toolbar.

Searching for Free Images in the Cricut Design Space

Several images are available to outsiders on the Cricut Access, the people who are not subscribed to the program. Cricut Design Space has undergone some modifications to simplify the search for images that the user requires from the sea of existing ones. Follow the instructions below to learn how to find these images at no cost:

Sign in to the Design Space and select "New Project." Proceed to click on "Images" and then the plus symbol near the "Ownership" text to enlarge the menu. Clicking on the "Free" box beneath the "Ownership" text will display the available free images. There are about 4,000 free images on Cricut Access, which will increase as time goes on.

To find images specific to your need, there is a search option that lets you enter a keyword related to what you need; this will ease the search and the stress of looking through hundreds of images. Furthermore, the image search also supports numerous filters. For example, selecting "Print Fill" will bring results of prints that you can cut in the Design Space. The number of filters that you already set can be found at the top and can also be cleared with a click on "Clear All."

The free images can be saved in an assignment in your Design Space account and cut for free. However, you have to pay for it or subscribe to Cricut Access to use the image if it is no longer available without charge before you can cut it.

The Weld Tool

The Weld Tool does a fine job of connecting multiple images into one design with no obvious seam line at the point of intersection. The Weld Tool works well for Linetype functions like "Score," "Draw," and "Cut" designs. However, both images must be identical, for example, Draw to Draw, Cut to Cut. The Linetypes do not work with written fonts. The modifications made by the Weld Tool to designs are not reversible after saving the design.

The Weld Tool is the second button from the left at the Layers Panel base, which is at the base corner on the right of the screen.

Functions of the Weld Tool

The Weld Tool can be used to join two images into a design without a cut line. It can also be used to make creations; there is no image that cannot be welded, even the Shapes menus free shapes. If you need a particular image that you do not have, check if it is possible to connect the ones you already have or any free ones to give you what you need.

The Weld Tool can also merge font scripts. Each letter will be cut separately instead of as a whole, cursive word when using font script; this happens even when you reduce each letter's spacing. What you can do to fix this is to ungroup the letter and then horizontally superimpose them to meet your preference. Proceed to highlight the letters and weld them to produce one cut.

The tool can be used to group images for the long run. One of the "Weld" Tool's primary functions is to fuse two individual images into one flawless piece that will be cut as one design. To make this function a notch higher, the tool can connect multiple images either in contact or not. This advanced function enables the tool to serve the "Group" option, though it is not reversible.

The tool can also expand borders and patterns. The majority of patterns and borders in the Cricut Design Space Library are small. Modification of the pattern size to make it longer warps the length or breadth. The Weld Tool is a perfect way of lengthening the designs without altering the measurements. To extend borders or patterns, superimpose multiple identical patterns or borders from end to end and then weld them.

To weld images, place the images you desire to weld on your canvas. The images will appear on separate lines in the right Layers Panel, which implies that they are distinctive individual cuts. Highlight the images and click on the Weld Tool; this action will erase superimposed lines to produce an image. The evidence that the images have been highlighted is the gray background on the Layers Panel.

To be sure that the images have been welded, you will discover that there is only one image, rather than multiple images, in the Layers Panel.

The Slice Tool

In simple terms, the Slice Tool cuts one image from another when two images are superimposed. The Slice Tool can perform Linetype functions like Draw, Cut, Score, and others. The only means of "cropping" images is using the Score Tool; this particular function is not reversible after saving.

Uses of the Slice Tool

It can cut one shape out of a design. It can also crop designs; the Cricut design space has no specific tool for cropping. The Circle or the Square from the shapes menu on the left toolbar work for rounded and straight-line crops. Modify the circle or square to your desired size and drag the re-sized shape on the design component you wish to crop. Mark the images and choose "Slice," then pull the images apart, and the component beneath the shape will be cut out. The remaining parts of the image that are not wanted can then be deleted.

The Slice Tool can cut designs to make them fit the cutting mat; big designs can be divided into smaller bits that fit a typical mat by applying the "Off the Mat" method.

The tool can also work for evening out designs with several layers. Slice the designs at the bottom layer to accurately space complex designs with multiple layers. To produce an even, accurately set design, deposit elevated layers on the empty openings.

Slicing in Cricut Design Space

A way to take out unwanted elements from a design or bring about an exceptional feel is by dividing an image.

Don't exceed two layers.

The Slice tool will not work if you are working with more than two layers per time, be it the layer of a file or an object. The Slice option will appear in the toolbar on the right side when you highlight two objects. The Slice tool will disappear when more than two objects are selected.

Place the one layer on the other in the manner that you would like the shape cut out; highlight the two objects and click on "Slice." After this, there will be a third layer in the toolbar on the right side, which is the layer that was just sliced.

Working with Slice Tool and Fonts

The slice tool also works amazingly with fonts. It helps to combine several objects, shapes, and letters into one object in a straightforward way. Bear in mind that only two objects can be sliced at once. After you have designed and you are satisfied with the kit, send it to cut.

Debugging

To fix the Slice Tool's problem, not marked selected designs, ensure that the images are not attached or grouped. Also, it is only possible to slice two images simultaneously, so it will require time and patience to slice severally on one design.

The Slice Tool is at the button on the extreme left, located at the Layers panel base. The panel is the corner button on the right of the screen.

The images you desire to slice should be placed on the canvas; the one you wish to cut out of the second one should be on top. To slice an image, highlight the items and click on the "Slice Tool." You will know the items are highlighted by the gray backdrop on the Layers Panel.

The action might not seem to make a difference on the canvas, but a close look at the Layers panel will tell you that the image is already sliced. To see that the base layer sliced the image on top, pull the layers apart.

Chapter 7: Key to Design Space

Rudimentary Tools

Tools are very important in every work; you can barely make progress without them. Every field of work has its own tools, so does the Design Space. Sometimes, the number of tools you use during your project can determine the beauty of your project output. There are so many tools in the Design Space, and we shall take a look at most of them and what they do.

Cricut Design Space Canvas Area

The reason for starting with the Canvas area is that all the arts and designing happen on this platform. The Canvas area is where you will be using your tools the most. You can easily carry out the organizing of your projects and the uploading of fonts and images here.

If you look closely, the Design Space is parallel with many other designing and editing programs people use out there. Programs such as Photoshop, Illustrator, and Adobe Creative Cloud are all similar to Cricut Design Space. Therefore, if you've got prior experience using programs like these, you shouldn't find it too challenging to flow with the Cricut Design Space.

Getting your membership for Cricut Access activated can help you design better and enhance your creativity.

Thus, the Canvas area is where your designs can be edited and perfected before cutting them. Nonetheless, there are several options to explore when working on the Canvas area, and you might get overwhelmed easily. So, we'll be discussing these options one after another, making their uses known as we proceed.

The Canvas area consists of four panes, which are the right panel, left panel, top panel, and the canvas area.

The Right Panel

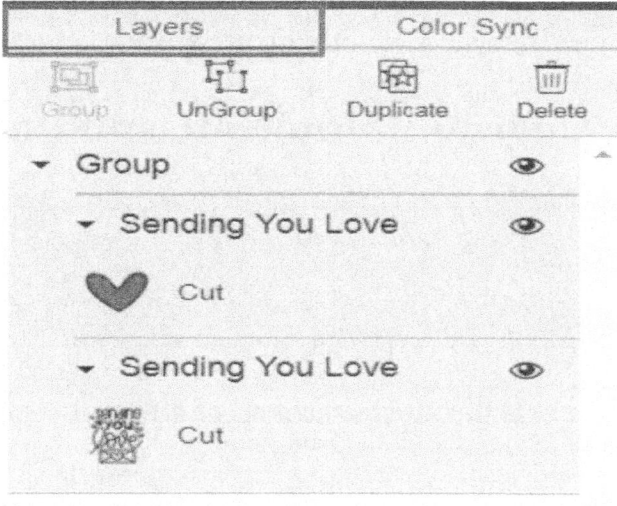

The Right panel is made up of layers; therefore, it's safe to call it the "Layers Panel." Layers indicate the designs present in the Canvas area. The number of layers you'll be using will be dependent on the intricacy of your project or design.

Take a birthday card, for example; you'll have different texts and decorations on it, and possibly one or two pictures. These are called the layers of your design.

This panel enables the creation and management of layers when a design is being made. All the items that are on the Layer Panel will show the Line type or Fill that you're using.

Group, Ungroup, Duplicate and Delete

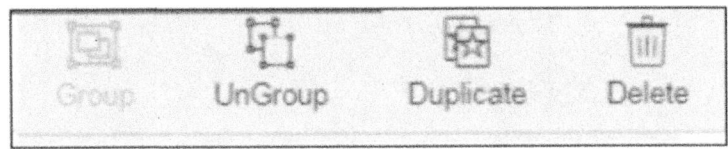

These tools enable the moving around of different designs on the Canvas area.

GROUP: This tool permits you to join or group different layers. When there are many layers that need to come together so as to form a design, then you can use the "Group" tool to bring everything together. For instance, if you are designing a house or building, there'll be diverse parts and sections in that building. A typical building should have a door, roof, windows, and walls. The Group tool will enable you to organize every layer and make sure that they all stay together whenever you are making the design.

UNGROUP: You can likewise detach a design that is made up of many layers by using the Ungroup tool. It simply does the opposite of what "Group" does.

DUPLICATE: This tool is self-explanatory. It simply duplicates whichever layer you choose on the Canvas.

DELETE: This tool gets rid of the layers you choose. It will delete it permanently away from the Canvas.

Blank Canvas

This layer is located on the Right panel. It enables you to modify the current Canvas color. If you are trying out different looks on your design, this option can be used to place your design against numerous backgrounds.

Layer Visibility

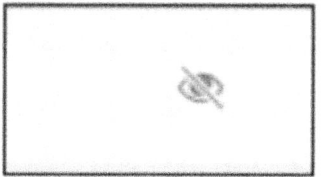

This icon in the image above indicates the visibility of your design or layer. You will find it on all layers on the Panel. It can be used when you're designing and you observe that a certain element or segment looks odd, you can then click on the icon to get it hidden. Doing that will make sure you do not end up removing it permanently in case you want it back later. Hidden items can be recognized with a visible cross mark.

Slice, Weld, Attach, Flatten, and Contour

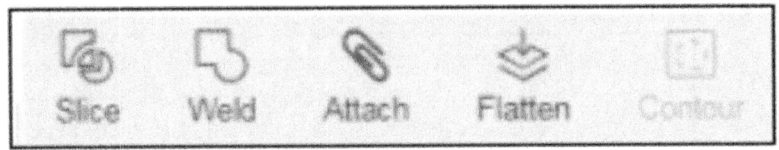

It is vital to study how to maximally utilize these 5 tools. They will always come in handy, regardless of whatever you are designing.

SLICE: Cricut made this tool for its users to carve out shapes, texts, and diverse elements from an entire design.

WELD: This is mainly used for merging shapes to form a new one. If you want to make something different or creative with your design, you can combine different shapes.

ATTACH: Attach is more like an advanced version of the "Group" tool. It joins shapes and modifies their colors to fit the background color you are using. These changes will still be in effect even after you're done cutting.

FLATTEN: This tool will be very useful when you're about printing different shapes. To flatten different shapes, select the layers you desire to print, and then pick the "Flatten" option.

CONTOUR: You can make use of this option if you desire to hide an entire layer or a small part of a layer of design. However, this can only be done when the layers in your design can be separated.

COLOR SYNC

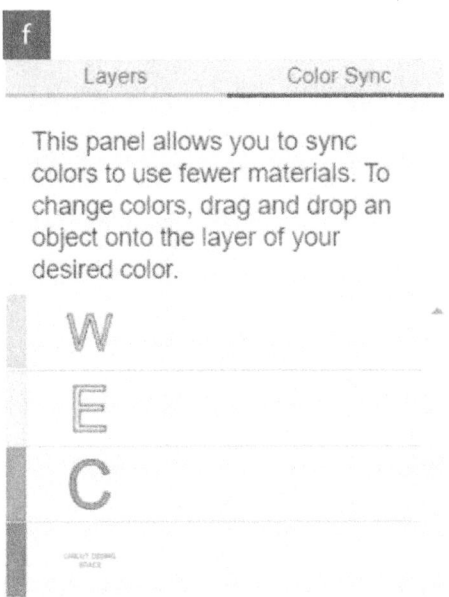

This tool is designed for balancing out your design and background colors. It can likewise be used to change diverse shades from a design color to a single color. As the name implies, Color Sync synchronizes the colors.

Left Panel

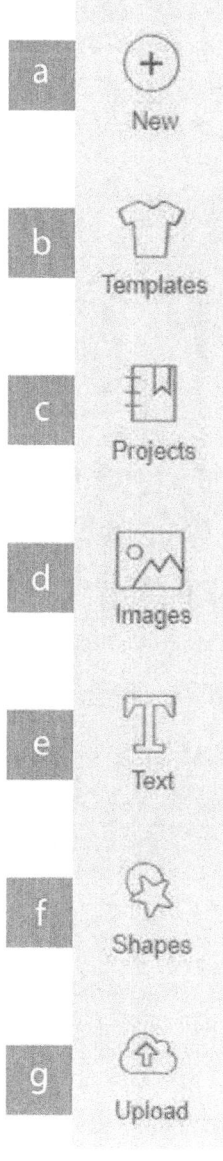

The Left Panel consists of every option needed for inserting. Shapes, images, texts, and even ready-to-cut projects can be added. With the Left Panel, you can insert everything you want to cut. The Left Panel has 7 options, let's quickly explore them all consecutively.

New

This option can be selected when you desire a new page. This new page is different from the page that you are designing with. It is better to save all your current designs before moving on to the page you just created. This is done to keep your designs in case you'll be needing them later. If you don't save before moving to the page you just created, your prior designs will be lost.

Templates

A template allows you to preview how your design is going to look like after cutting it out on a specific kind of fabric such as a bag or a t-shirt. If you are making a bag with an iron-on design, it'll show you an image of your bag, and the design can now be placed on that template so that you can start planning the appearance of the bag in reality.

Templates will not cut out a real backpack for you, but they'll give you a clue of what the designs look like when they are cut out.

Projects

If you are ready to start cutting, then go to "Projects." You'll choose your project, make edits, modify it to suit your taste, and then click the "Make It" option. There are several projects that are available for users with Cricut Access membership, and some projects are accessible by purchase only. Apart from both means, only a few projects are free.

Images

Images enable you to spice up your designs by adding a personal touch. With this tool, you are able to insert images that are provided on the Design Space for you. Cricut even offers free pictures each week, though some of them come with the Cricut Access.

Text

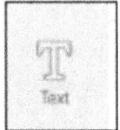

The text tool enables you to include texts to your designs or simply on the Canvas area. Clicking the "Text" tool opens a little window, indicating that you should add your text. You can add a text and also customize the color and font.

Shapes

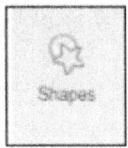

This tool is used when you wish to add a shape to your Canvas area. The Design Space provides some shapes for its users, namely; square, triangle, hexagon, pentagon, heart, star, and octagon.

There is likewise the "Score Line" tool located under the "Shapes" option. You can utilize this tool for folding these shapes to form other diverse shapes, particularly when you're making cards.

Upload

The "Upload" tool is the last tool you will find in the Left Panel. This tool enables you to carry out file and image uploads, excluding the ones provided by Cricut. With this, images and patterns can be uploaded.

Elementary Functions

Functions and tools are almost the same thing. You can know the functions of a tool and you can know the function of a function. However, what I regard as functions in the design space are options that are used for making edits, organizing, or tweaking the Canvas area. Let us proceed and check out some of the general functions of the Cricut Design Space.

Top Panel

The Top Panel is the only pane that is always full of activities. There are two different sub-panels under the Top Panel. Generally, the Top Panel is for organizing and making general editing on layers of design and elements.

First Subpanel

This enables a user to name their projects, save them, and finally cut it. In this subpanel, you can also find the options to save, name, and send your project for cutting on the Cricut machine.

TOGGLE MENU: This option enables you to perform account and subscription management. This menu likewise allows you to update your Design Space, calibrate your Cricut machine, and perform some other operations.

PROJECT NAME: Apparently, you can use this function to name your project. The project's default name will be "Untitled," it will always be like that until you rename it to something unique you can identify the project with.

MY PROJECTS: This serves as a library for all your saved projects on the Design Space. So, this makes it possible to access old projects easily.

SAVE: This option gets your project saved into the Design Space Library. You should always save your work so you won't have issues when your browser crashes or stops responding.

CRICUT MAKER / CRICUT EXPLORE: When using the Design Space for the first time, a question will pop up to inquire if you're making use of a Cricut Explore machine from the Series or a Cricut Maker. Cricut Maker stands as the most advanced machine made by Cricut, and therefore, it provides several benefits on the Design Space more than other machines you will find in the Explore Series.

MAKE IT: Click "Make It" after you have uploaded your files so that it can start cutting. The software categorizes your projects based on their colors, and if you are making plans to cut two or more projects, you can use this tool to increment the projects you wish to cut.

Second Subpanel

The second subpanel is a menu for editing. It enables you to arrange, organize, and edit fonts and images on the canvas area.

UNDO & REDO

Clicking "Undo" will revert a recent activity or action, and it is mostly used when a mistake is made or when an undesired move has been made. "Redo" does the opposite of "Undo," it brings back a deleted or reverted activity or action, and it is mostly used when something needed has been mistakenly deleted.

Chapter 8: How to Create Different Objects

Inserting Images from Cricut Image Library

Cricut Design Space has over 70,000 images, as more are being added weekly. Even if you don't own an image yet it doesn't call for worry because Design Space allows you to Design an image before you finally buy one to ensure that it will work on your project.

Tips: The relativeness of an image depends on your licensing agreement and your residential address. Image tiles are shown in 2 different sizes to enable you to view more images at once or to get more details about each image. To go through all selected images, swipe to left or to right in the image tray at the bottom of the panel. If you no longer desire an image on display, tap that particular image once or twice on the thumbnail in the image tray.

Step I: Hit on the Design tab button to enable you to go to the Design canvas or "Start a new project from scratch."

Step II: Hit on the image button to enable the image panel to open.

Step III: To go through the image tiles, move your finger up or down.

Step IV: The Insert Image panel allows you to view and search for images in the Cricut Image Library.

Step V: Hit on any image you wish to use; the place mark will display in the right-hand corner of the tile showing that it has been selected by you. A thumbnail of the image will display in the image tray close to the bottom of the Insert Image panel.

Step VI: Hit on the "insert" button to add all images in the tray that has been selected on the design screen, or hit on "cancel" to reverse back to the design screen without accomplishing any image insertion.

Inserting an Image

While in the Design canvas, the following are ways you insert an image into your Design Space:

Step I: Open the file you wish to edit or you are already working on.

Step II: To upload your own images, click on select Uploads.

Step III: Select any image you wish to upload and give it time to finish uploading.

Step IV: Select the image to insert into your design.

Step V: Drag the image to increase or decrease fit into your design.

Searching for Images

Step I: If the App you are using is in Android/iOS, tap the image button at the bottom left-hand side of the screen, or click images on the left-hand side of the design screen using Windows/Mac computer.

Step II: While you are here, you can browse, search, and filtered needed images.

Step III: You can now search "All Images" View featured images or search for a particular image as surf the entire Cricut Library.

Browsing Images by Category

Tips: Every filter and Category tags usually display in a horizontal scroll list above the image thumbnails. If you want to cancel or clear a filter or category tag, tap on the X symbol next to the tag. But if you clear all of them, you can tap on the "Reset All" button on the right-hand part of the list.

Step I: Begin browsing image categories as you tap the "Categories" menu on the left-hand side of the Insert Image panel.

Step II: Ensure you choose as many categories and sub-categories as you want. Every category you choose will be automatically added to the total number of images you have chosen. As soon as you add a category, its tag will display at the top of the image tiles region.

Step III: As soon as you have selected those images, tap the "Insert" button to send them to the design screen.

How to Browse and Search for Cartridges

During your project creation, you may wish to use designs from Cartridges. Images from Cartridges always come with a similar design, which will help make your projects more attractive. Purchasing a whole cartridge can be a very great cost-saving compared to purchasing individual images.

Step I: Click on the images Tab in the Design Panel on the left-hand side of the canvas, to view various categories of cartridges, you will start by entering the Cricut Image Library.

Step II: An entirely new window will pop up having the Image Library. To browse in alphabetical order a list of about 500 Cartridges, click on the screen.

Step III: At this time, all views will change showing a list of every Cricut Cartridges, every one of them is represented by a tile in a horizontal form. With the Cartridge, tile is the Cartridge name and the sample represents its images. On the right-hand side, is the number of images contained in that Cartridge and your level of accessibility, which includes free, purchased, and subscribe or a price tag for purchase.

Step IV: By clicking on view all images located at the right-hand corner of the Cartridges Tile, the system will be able to showcase all images available within a cartridge.

Step V: You will see a text in the search bar which implies that you are only searching within this cartridge. If you want to search for a particular image in the cartridge; just type in the search bar and click on the magnifying lens.

Step VI: The outcome will be a display of images available in the cartridge that was tagged with your search word. As soon as those images are selected, click on the button "Insert Images" to include them to the canvas.

Step VII: The final stage of this search is to move them about and sizing them to have a view of how they may look on your project.

Inserting Basic Shapes

To insert Basic Shapes in your Cricut Design Space or your Design Canvas, you need a Design Space compatible Cricut Machine (either an Explore or the Maker) that allows you to draw with pens. The steps below will guide you through as you insert basic shapes of your choice whether you are using a desktop computer or a laptop computer. But if the app is to be used on mobile devices, it is not that the buttons and tools will be found in entirely different locations on your screen, but the features are the same for all devices.

Step I: Sign in to Cricut Design Space Using design.cricut.com

You will log in using your Cricut ID and password, after which you will now select the green button "New Project" located at the top right-hand side.

Step II: Insert and Resize a Basic Shape (square)

If you want to form the base of the design, you will insert a square shape by clicking on the shapes located on the left-hand side of the screen. Then add a square to your canvas.

Step III: Color the Square with as Many Colors as You Want

Located at the Edit bar, next to the Line type is the colored square, select and change the color of the item to white. I chose to work with white because I'm going to use it on Daisy cardstock as a base for my design, it enables the pattern to be easily seen as you work on your canvas.

Step IV: Insert and Ungroup the Triangular Flag as you Delete the Remaining Shape

From the "You Are Here Collection," click images to add new images to the canvas. Use #M282C66F to search for images to be added to your canvas. Click on the flag and choose to Ungroup in the layers panel at the right-hand side. As soon as you have demarcated the shape into two images, you are now free to delete the purple flag.

Step V: Resize, Duplicate, and Flip the Triangle

The width and height of the triangle should be resized to 1. Design Space will only allow you to modify both images if you unlock them. Select the triangle and click Duplicate in the Layers Panel. To flip shapes, select the second triangle, go to Flip in the Edit bar, and select Flip Vertically.

Step VI: Arrange and Group both Triangles

Position the two triangles vertically, leaving a little space between them. Click the first triangle, hold on to the shift key on your keyboard, and click the second triangle. Choose the option Group in the Layers Panel.

Step VII: Make Duplicates of the Triangles and Arrange in a Row

You can arrange these shapes in the center by first selecting all sets of five duplicated triangles. For example, in 8 steps, this can be done by holding on to the shift key on your keyboard. Then select the option "Center Horizontally" under Align in the Edit bar.

Step VIII: Make a Duplicate of the Triangular Row Eight Times

You need eight rows, having a little atom of space between each one of them.

Step IX: Match the Top and Bottom Rows of Triangles

Use the Ungroup button in the Layers Panel to separate the bottom set of triangles and move the last triangle from the bottom of the design to the top, which should be when you notice that part of the design isn't going to match on the white square.

Step X: Change Cut to Draw and Add Pen Color

Now that your first set of triangles is ready, you can also change the Linetype in the Edit bar from Cut to Draw. After which, you click on the box next to Draw. This is where you select the pen size and color.

Step XI: Group Eight Rows of Colored Triangles Together and Duplicate

Click and move your cursor over the rows. Then closely cluster the rows and duplicate. Move the new group of triangles next to the first one, maintaining a reasonable space between them.

Step XII: Jointly Group All Rows of Colored Triangles

After the grouping, align and attach to the white square. Then select both the white square and the grouped triangles. Under align, you now click Center. The triangles on the square will be centered. After this, you select Attach at the bottom of the Layers Panel. This enables your shapes to draw just the way you have arranged them on the square.

Step XIII: Cut and Draw Your Project

As soon as you are set to draw the design and cut the material, click on the Make It green button in the upright corner and follow the instructions. Ensure you load the right pen color to Clamp A of the Cricut. If you are thinking about the right pen to use, don't worry about that because Design Space will do that for you, just as your machine draws the design, it will urge you to move to the next color. At the end of the design, you will have a bright multicolor background.

Working with Images

There are two major ways whereby we do select images on the design screen, which are selecting a single image or selecting multiple images.

Selecting a Single Image

Step I: Go straight to the image and click on it. The bounding box appearing around the edges of the image indicates that such an image has been selected.

Step II: The image manipulation handles will display too. By this, you can resize, delete, rotate, and lock/unlock the area for the selected image.

Selecting Multiple Images

Step I: Tap twice on an empty space of the design screen. This enables it to zoom in or out to display all images.

Step II: Swiping either left or right allows you to create a selection box that covers all the images you want to select. The selection box is shaded light blue.

Chapter 9: Tips and Tricks for Design Space

Now, you have got familiar with all the tools and options that Cricut Design Space offers. However, practice is what will make you perfect. When I started using Design Space, I was also overwhelmed. Moreover, I didn't even have a book or platform that would provide me with complete guidance about this software's usage. I watched hundreds of videos and tutorials literally to get the hang of it. Still, I was not perfect. However, with practice, trial and error, I mastered it. Here, I am going to share some hacks that I have learned on my own.

Search by Synonym

It becomes a lot easier when you find your desired images from the Cricut image search option. It saves you from the hassle of creating an entire project yourself. However, what if you don't find the relevant image? I went through this problem when I started using Design Space as a beginner. I would spend the entire day creating my designs and still wouldn't get the perfect results. However, this problem was resolved when I started searching for my desired images using different synonyms. Searching by synonyms helps because every image is tagged with various search phrases. When you use relevant synonyms, you get better results. For example, when I want to search for a heart image, I use all appropriate terms to get the best results, such as heart, love, valentine, and more.

Get More Images from the Image Set

When searching for images, we see one particular idea that seems to be the most relevant. We wish to see more photos like this, but we cannot find them. However, there is a trick that will help you get similar shots. The best place to start is with the set it came from. Just click the small information icon (I) in the bottom right corner of the image you like. It will open up the image details. See figure, I searched for flowers and clicked the (I) icon of the image I wanted the most. Now, I will click "View Image Sets" to see similar images.

This image set has 50 similar images. Now you can work with a lot more options.

Get Free Images and Text

Getting a Cricut Access subscription is quite useful if you are a regular or, I should say, professional crafter. However, many times, people don't want to spend money on these images and text, especially when they are beginners and just practicing cutting on their machine. If you are also a newbie and don't want to spend money, for now, you don't need to worry. Design Space also offers various free images that you can play with even if you don't have a Cricut Access subscription.

To enjoy free images, click "Ownership" in the left side Filters panel. You will find four options. Click "Free."

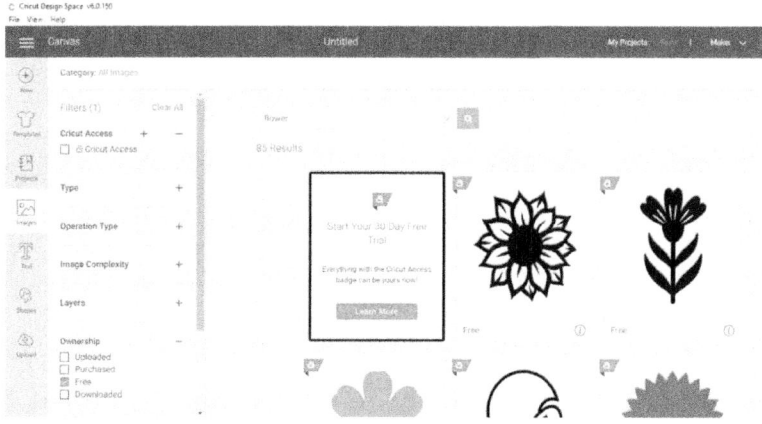

Now, whatever you search for, Design Space will only show you free results.

Enjoy Free Fonts

When you type a text in Cricut Design Space and want to change the font style, it gives you the option to download premium fonts for your customized designs other than already installed system fonts. You feel tempted to download these fonts but don't want to spend money, right? I have a solution for this as well. The internet is full of some unique free fonts. You can search for free fonts on Google, download, and enjoy. Follow the next steps:

1. Search for the fonts.
2. Download it.
3. Find the zipped file (.zip) on your computer.
4. Unzip it.
5. Click on the font folder.
6. Click on font file (.otf or .ttf).
7. Click Install.

Once you are done with installing the fonts, close the Cricut Design Space, restart it and have fun with new fonts.

Remove Gridlines

Have you ever wanted to see how your project design looks without the Design Space canvas's grid lines? Well, this is not something impossible. You can easily remove these gridlines and bring them back whenever you want.

Look at the circled square. When you click this square once, all the gridlines will disappear. By clicking the square again, you will only see bigger grids.

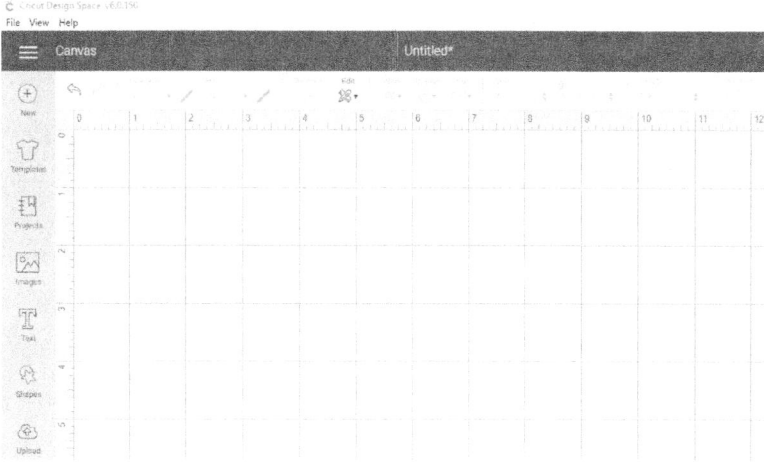

When you click the same square for the third time, all the grids will reappear.

Change Any Line to Cut, Score or Draw

It's is a fantastic option that many Design Space users are not familiar with. When you insert an image from Cricut Access or draw a shape, the default line type is "cut." However, we often want these designs or shapes removed (using a pen) or scored (using a scoring stylus) instead of being cut. You can do it only by changing the line type. Insert the image or draw the shape of your choice. Select that design, and in the editing toolbar at the top, change the line type to "draw" or "score."

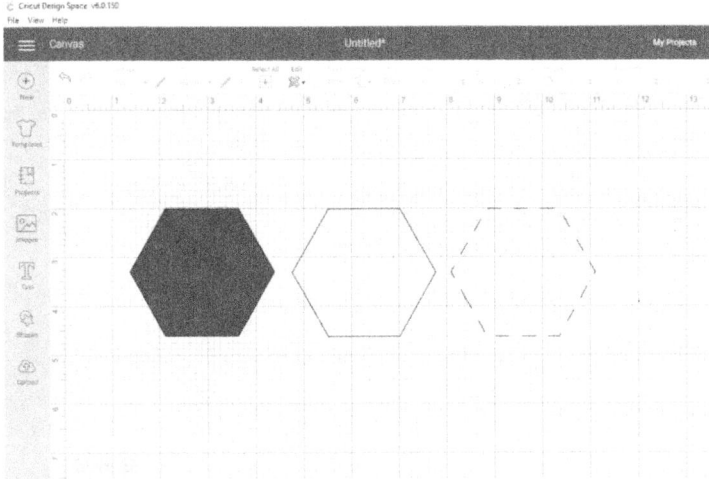

Play with Patterns

It's is another fantastic feature that will enhance the quality of your project. Most of the time, when we are creating projects, we use cardstock or patterned scrapbook paper. However, you cannot manipulate these patterns according to your choice. What if you don't want to rely on scrapbook paper patterns and create something on your own? Design Space comes in handy in such a situation as well. In the editing toolbar at the top, there is the option "fill." By default, it is set to "no fill." However, when you click it, the drop-down menu allows you to change its type to "print."

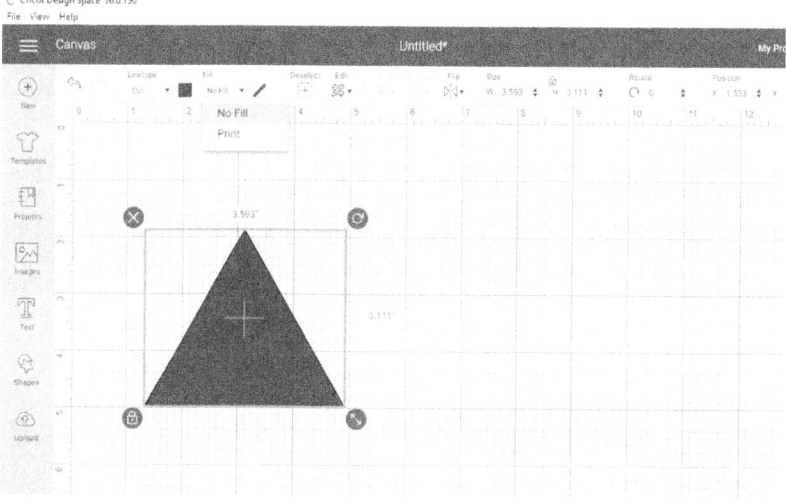

When you select "print," the color fill option (little crossed square) next to it becomes active. Click this option and from there go to "patterns."

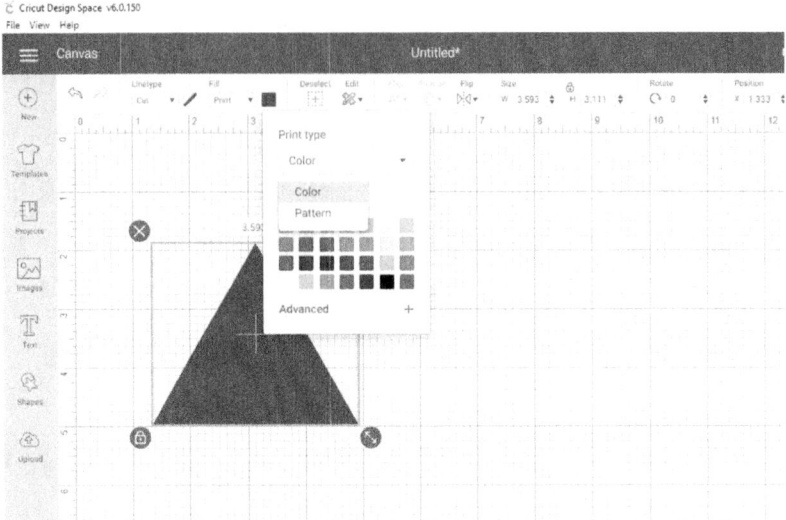

Clicking on "patterns" will give you various pre-loaded Design Space patterns that you can play with. You can even edit the size and dimensions of these patterns by using the "Edit Pattern" option.

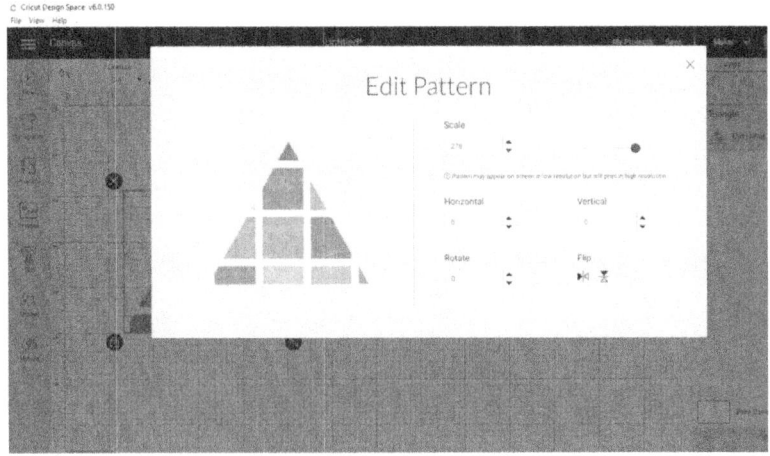

Once you have finalized your customized pattern, first print it using your printer and then place the printed design on Cricut Mat to cut it as usual.

Move Things on Your Mat

Has it ever happened to you that after clicking the "Make It" button, you suddenly want to make some change to your design? What do you do in such a situation? Probably, you go back to the canvas and make changes. However, the good news is that you can do a variety of things on the cut screen itself without having to go back to your canvas. For example, you can transfer items around on the mat. Only by dragging and then dropping the pictures you can move a design to be cut anyplace on the mat and even switch it. This is especially useful when the material you are using has some odd pattern, and you want your design to be cut on a particular position on the mat.

Connect Several Machines Simultaneously

I know most people don't have more than one model of Cricut Machine. However, if you have, you can connect all the machines to your Design Space account through Bluetooth or USB. I know you must be puzzled as to which device your images will go for cutting. You don't need to worry about it. No matter how many devices are connected to your Design Space, on the final cut screen, you can always choose your desired machine from the drop-down menu and cut your design the way you want.

Change Cut Settings for Your Materials

One problem that most beginners face is that their Cricut doesn't cut through it properly despite setting their machine to specific material. They think it happens because of the quality of the material. However, in most cases, this is not the reason. You can resolve this issue by adjusting settings for any material. Let's see how you can do it.

- If you are using Cricut Maker, on the Cut Screen, you will have the option to select "Materials."
- Then select Browse All Materials.
- At the bottom of this menu, you will find the "Material Settings" option.

From there, you can select any material and adjust the settings about the number of passes the machine should make and the depth of each pass.

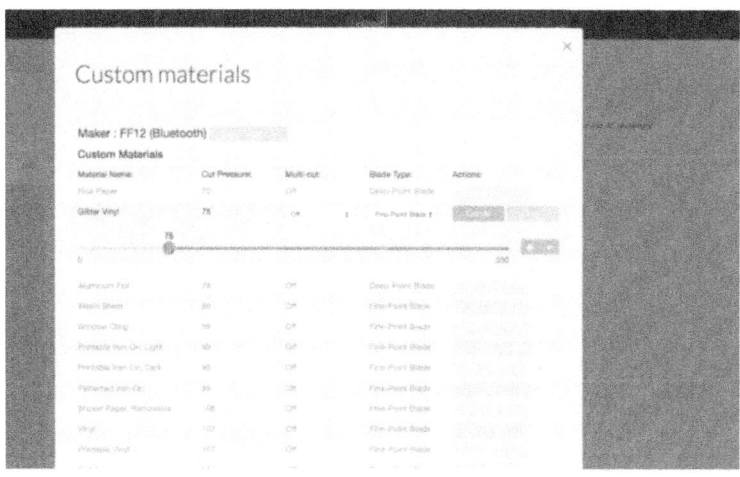

Adjust Cut Pressure

Design Space also allows you to adjust the Cut pressure for your material without struggling with in-depth settings. When you select your material on the final cut screen, it provides a drop-down menu to adjust the Cut pressure. You can choose either Default, More, or Less depending on your material's thickness and depth. It will allow your material to be cleanly cut through.

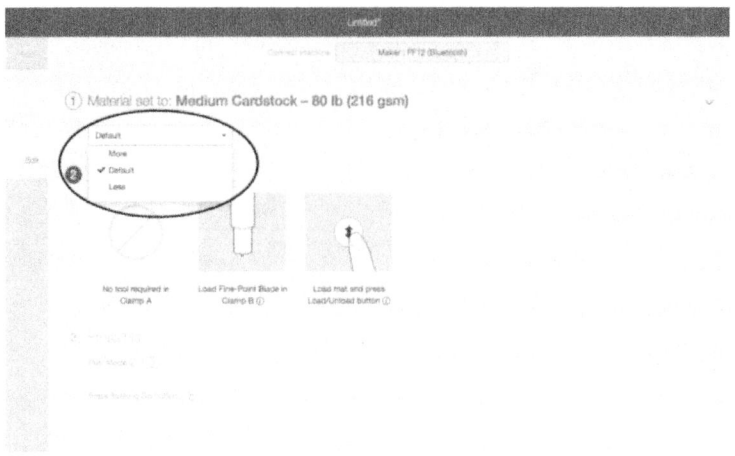

Change the Size of Your Mat

Design Space also allows you to change your material's size according to the nature and requirement of your project. You can do this through the "Material Size" option on the cut screen.

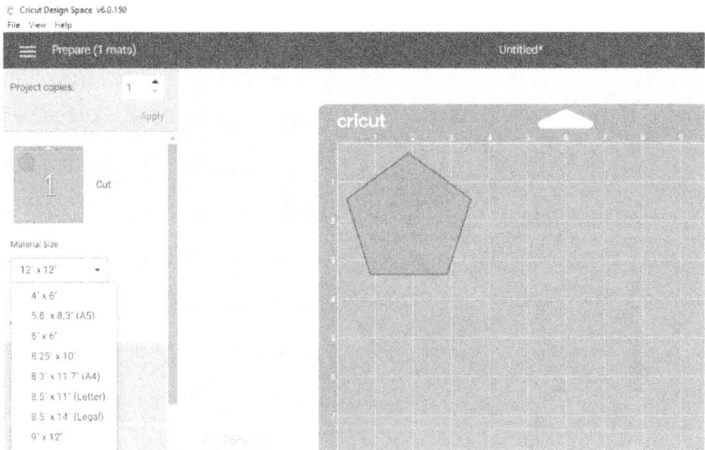

These were some of the hacks that I learned with practice, trial and error. I am sure you can discover more once you get the hangs of this magic software and machine.

Conclusion

Cricut Design Space is a new DIY workspace for Cricut Cartridges. It's the easiest way to design and cut your projects to fit any of your favorite Cricut Cartridges.

Cricut Design Space is a great tool for those who already have a Cricut machine or those who are curious about getting one. You can choose from over 500 popular SVG files, upload your own designs and images, trim them to size instantly, drag-and-drop onto the appropriate cartridge templates, and then easily download all the files in one click.

The benefits of Cricut Design Space include:

- Use your favorite graphics tools, such as Photoshop, to design projects for cutting. Cricut Design Space is compatible with most major graphics tools including the free Adobe ® Photoshop ® Elements software. It is not necessary to learn a new software program. Use the one you already know and love!

- Cut projects in any shape or size with no limitations on either your machine or Design Space. With our new advanced layering system, you can cut projects using a wide variety of materials including paper, fabric, vinyl, and other specialty papers.
- Connect and share your amazing projects with Cricut's online Design Space community.
- You can also open an account for Cricut Design Space.

How to Use it?

1. Download Design Space by visiting the online store at https://cricutdesignspace.myshopify.com/
2. Create your account and then log in to Design Space
3. Select an image you wish to use, open it, and drag-and-drop it into the workspace
4. Name your design and add a description of what it is made out of (specialty paper, vinyl, etc.)
5. Click "create project" in Design Space or download the SVG file directly from Design Space
6. Print to cutting machine software, cut, and then enjoy your awesome projects!

Here are some practical tips in using Cricut Design Space:

1. Upload an image to Design Space

2. Use the sizing tool to create a vector for cutting with your Cricut machine
3. Use the text tool to type words in your project
4. Add lines and shapes to enhance your project
5. Upload a project template from one of the 500+ existing SVG projects or download an existing design on Design Space for importing into your project

I hope that this book had helped you to learn more about Design Space and give you some guidance to using it.

Always remember that when doing a Cricut project, you must have a strong patience. It's not going to be easy every time.

CRICUT PROJECTS

BOOST YOUR IMAGINATION AND CREATIVITY TO CREATE WONDERFUL PROJECTS AND AMAZE YOUR FAMILY AND FRIENDS

Samuel Blade

Introduction

We should not forget that the cool thing about Cricut is that projects are endless. You might decide to have your own wall lettering, or you might choose to make a nursery at home, and you would need to make that distinct wall painting with several letters. Instead of spending several hours cutting with blades and carving with knives or any other cutting device, you just need a Cricut machine. You do not even need to hire a muralist for your hand painting because you can do that yourself. In fact, people like these are happy that you are not exposed to this knowledge so that they can make some cash from you. The die-cutting machine produces those precise cuts that children and other professionals need. There are several die-cut stickers you can get from this machine. This machine also allows you to render wedding favors and party favors easily by helping in the creating process of tags, bags, boxes, and several other party creations. These pieces can come in several forms like gift bags, banners, hats, etc., these and many more can fit the theme of any party because you are making them. As much as I would love to shy away from the scrapbook stuff, I just cannot. Now, just picture your daughter or your son getting married and you present him/her with a scrapbook having pictures from the very first day they stepped into this planet to where they are now. Gifts like this sound odd, but they are invaluable because you are not giving out a utensil or a tool, you are giving out those memories. Scrapbooks carry out a lot of memories and those feelings you cannot give through your regular gifts.

If you have a Cricut machine and you have not gotten these supplies, I would advise that you get them as soon as possible. We are aware that these supplies are grouped into different categories. First is the paper category which includes; adhesive cardstock, cereal box, copy paper, flocked paper, cardboard paper, Notebook paper, flocked cardstock, foil embossed paper, Freezer Paper, Glitter Paper, Kraft paper, Kraft Board, metallic Paper, Metallic Posterboard, Photographs, Poster Board, Rice Paper, Solid core Cardstock, Wax Paper, Photo Framing Mat, White Core Cardstock, Photo Framing mat, Watercolor Paper, Freezer Paper, Foil Poster Board, etc.

We should not forget that Vinyl is another material that you need to make your work on the Cricut machine smooth. The Cricut machine can work on those beautiful materials that can be used to make decals, stencils, graphics, and those beautiful signs too. You can cut through the following vinyl materials, chalkboard vinyl, dry erase vinyl, holographic vinyl, stencil vinyl, printable vinyl, Matte Vinyl, Adhesive Vinyl, Printable Vinyl, and Glossy

Vinyl too. Furthermore, you may have so much experience in the fabric and Textile world, and you want to infuse the Cricut machine. Some of the materials or fabrics that you can work with are; canvas, denim, cotton fabric, linen, leather, flannel, burlap, duck cloth, felt, metallic leather, polyester, printable fabrics, silk, wool felt, and many more others if you have not got your Iron on Vinyl. Which is meant to be the heat transfer vinyl. You make use of this vinyl to decorate a T-shirt, tote bags and other kinds of fabric items that you can think of like; Printable Iron On, Glitter Iron on, Glossy Iron On, Flocked Iron on, Holographic sparkle iron on, Metallic Iron on, Neon Iron on, Foil Iron on, etc.

We should not narrow our minds to the materials mentioned above because there are several other materials that the Cricut can cut through or even work on, some of them include; adhesive wood, corkboard, Balsa Wood, craft foam, aluminum sheets, corrugated paper, Embossable foil, Foil Acetate, Paint Chips, Plastic Packaging, Metallic Vellum, Printable Sticker Paper, Stencil material, Shrink Plastic, Wrapping Paper, Window Cling, Wood Veneer, Washi Tape, Birch Wood, Wrapping Paper, Wood Veneer, Plastic Packaging, Soda Can, Glitter Foam, Printable Magnet Sheets, etc. The Cricut maker can work on materials that are up to 2.4mm thick and other special materials and special fabrics like; Jersey, Cashmere, Chiffon, Terry Cloth, Tweed, Velvet, Jute, Knits, Moleskin, Fleece, and several others.

This machine can be found everywhere, so much paper artwork is done. What this suggests is that you can see these machines in schools, offices, craft shops, etc. You can make use of this Cricut machine for a school project, card stock projects and iron-on projects too. Making use of this machine to cut out window clings is not a bad idea at all. It is not limited to this because you also engage in projects that have to do with an adhesive stencil and stencil vinyl. You would remove the stencil vinyl after it is dried. This would leave a distinct imprint. You can also make use of this machine to create lovely fashion accessories like several pieces of jewelry. The Cricut machine allows you to use faux leather for exceptional designs. Recall that we talked about school projects. Preschoolers and their instructors can benefit from this machine. Furthermore, you can print out photos or images from your computer while making use of this machine, especially from the printable magnets to those sticker papers, customized gifts, bags, etc.

Defining objects requires you to use other similar objects to drive home your point and to give the reader a clearer picture. The very available way we can describe a Cricut machine is to say that it is a machine that has so much resemblance with the printer, but it is used majorly for cutting designed pieces. That is a very simple and easy definition you do not need to bother yourself about that. Just picture a printer in your mind and think of a cutting device.

Oh, no, you already have the Cricut machine with you, right? You would notice that it uses precise blades and several templates or rollers during cutting.

Against what people think, the machine is not meant for scrapbook keepers or makers alone. I still do not know why this idea has become so much rooted in the minds of people that we have grown to allow this thought to dominate our reactions and attitude towards any new innovation.

The world has been transformed with that machine as its products have been able to add those special visual beauties to the simple paperwork that we know. The Cricut machine has several models and versions, some of them include Cricut Expression, Expression 2, Cricut Imagine, Cricut Gypsy, Cricut Cake Mini, Cricut Personal Cutter, Cricut Crafts Edition and Martha Stewart, and the Cricut Explore Air. The tool obviously fits into any type of craft you are working on. And there is also a die-cutting machine that gives you that extra-precise, sharp, and smart cutting. The process of cutting materials by hand during crafts has been reduced drastically, thanks to this wonderful machine. Additionally, you can perform multiple projects all at the same time due to the effectiveness of this device. It contains several cartridges that are always available to help you explore different forms and shapes of several designs. Also, that move from one project to another has been made possible with the use of this Cricut machine.

Any material can be shaped into that design you want it to be. Furthermore, you can also create patterns that are already pre-installed in the software that comes with it. The design software tool becomes very much available with pre-loaded designs for instant use. I am sure you must have been able to purchase this machine from your local craft store or the online store. You are aware that the price was based on the kind of model you are using and I am sure that you've been able to narrow down your needs for you to be able to get your machine because anything which makes your work easier and faster is a very important investment and the Cricut machine is definitely one. Due to the efficiency of this machine, we now have it in several places we never thought it would be in years. We have them in offices and specific workshops. If you think that the Cricut is a home-only tool, you are quite wrong. This time-saving device allows your work to be very professional, and the beautiful thing about it is that we have no limits to what it can do. I am sure that you are reading this to gain more ideas and you hastily want to jump into making things and doing some stuff. Yes, that is cool; however, we need to understand some basics. Otherwise, we would be making serious mistakes or the process would look very confusing.

Chapter 1: Cricut Projects You Can Make

500 Cricut Ideas to Spark Your Imagination

The possibilities with your Cricut are nearly infinite. We could fill an entire library with project instructions! Instead of doing that, look through this list of words and phrases, and see what they spark in your mind. You could use them as project titles and create something that fits it, or it could be the inspiration that lets you come up with something completely different. Here are 500 more ideas to inspire you. Take these phrases and create a project with them!

1. Pet food and water bowls
2. Kitchen dry goods storage
3. Pool toys
4. Holiday mug
5. Etched casserole dish
6. Custom cooking utensils
7. Quote sweatshirt

8. Patterned tiles
9. Giant wall art
10. Paper banners
11. Paper sculptures
12. Vinyl Christmas tree
13. Treat bags
14. Party favors
15. Cake decorations
16. Gift boxes
17. Custom kid's ornaments
18. Party place settings
19. Origami
20. Handmade cards
21. Bookmarks
22. Refrigerator magnets
23. Chalkboards
24. Dry erase labels
25. Music picture frame
26. Desk organizer
27. Easter baskets
28. Personalized tools
29. Etched Mason jars
30. Wine or champagne glass markers
31. Canvas art

32. Decorative plates
33. Ice cream bowls
34. Party games
35. Halloween masks
36. Wine bottle lamps
37. Valentines
38. Candy holders
39. Wooden signs
40. Beach bag
41. Drink holders
42. Mug warmers
43. Pencil pouch
44. Calligraphy wall art
45. Customized lap desk
46. Breakfast-in-bed tray
47. Coffee bar sign
48. Cookie jar
49. Crafting stamps
50. Planner stickers
51. Custom calendar
52. Journal pages
53. Welcome mat
54. Wine gift bag
55. Silhouette art

56. Art storage
57. Labeled laundry baskets
58. Customized travel mugs
59. State silhouette signs
60. Forest themed nursery décor
61. Candle holders
62. Custom shot glasses
63. Wedding favors
64. Book tote bag
65. Patterned wood letters
66. Quilled art
67. Team t-shirts
68. Teacher appreciation mug gifts
69. Photo booth props
70. Personalized bottle cap catcher
71. Wine cork box
72. Paper succulents
73. Patterned scarf
74. Designed umbrella
75. Mandala hoodie
76. 3D stars
77. Doll clothing
78. Custom jigsaw puzzle
79. Glitter tumblers

80. Labeled pantry bins
81. Kitchen conversions chart
82. Family center
83. Paper straw party decorations
84. Headbands
85. Personalized tea towels
86. Stained glass wind chime
87. Ring dish
88. Monogrammed throw pillow
89. Giant bows
90. Kitchen mixer decals
91. Custom onesies
92. Car window decals
93. Hanging planter
94. Bumper stickers
95. Paper flower wreath
96. Nursery mobile
97. Food pun dish towels
98. Customized beach towel
99. Drink cooler
100. Pendant necklace
101. Leather tassel earrings
102. Finger puppets
103. 3D puzzles

104. Charity shirts
105. Glass cutting board
106. Wooden family name sign
107. Notebook covers
108. Flip flops
109. Decorative hand mirror
110. Makeup storage
111. Pop up paper animals
112. Felt flowers
113. Quilts
114. Vinyl banners
115. Custom pot holders
116. Thank you cards
117. Leather purse
118. Dry erase weekly menu
119. Cookies for Santa plate and mug
120. Family tree wall art
121. Photo magnets
122. Window clings
123. Felt headband
124. Tupperware for food gifts
125. Sleep mask
126. Microwaveable rice pack
127. Leather cuff bracelet

128. Custom ballcaps
129. Decorated dog bandanas
130. Tooth fairy bags
131. Coloring books
132. Pop up cards
133. Polka dot vase
134. Winter shadowbox
135. Drink koozies
136. Custom drawer pulls
137. Photo board
138. Planner pages
139. Balsa wood jewelry
140. Etched pet tags
141. Water measurement bottle
142. Etched measuring glass
143. Countdown sign
144. Workout tank top
145. Large wall decals
146. Embossed cards
147. Chipboard letters
148. Striped coffee mug
149. Tea bag holder
150. Decorative tea light holders
151. Foam stamps

152. Llama mask
153. Price tags
154. Paper pinwheels
155. Address labels
156. Faux leather initial pendant
157. Felt flower hair clip
158. Earring cards
159. Treat packaging
160. Paper lanterns
161. Baby milestone blanket
162. Cupcake gift box
163. Custom mittens
164. Silhouette candle jar
165. Wood name keychain
166. Faux leather luggage tag
167. Paper cut art
168. School year backpack
169. Hangry apron
170. Father's Day cake topper
171. Galaxy coasters
172. Wedding table numbers
173. Passport holder
174. Nightlight cover
175. Foodie lunch box

176. Paper fans
177. Geometric canvas art
178. Pencil roll
179. Growth chart
180. Classroom bulletin board
181. Patterned phone case
182. Seasonal placemats
183. Child's handprint art
184. Dog/cat collar decorations
185. Memory match game
186. Dog/cat bed
187. Napkin rings
188. Christmas stockings
189. Party menus
190. Leather flower keychain
191. Sticker sheets
192. Custom craft apron
193. Pegboard organization
194. Chore chart
195. Shabby chic sign
196. Shoe bins
197. Stamped leather bracelet
198. Dreamcatcher canvas
199. Quote phone case

200. Stuffed felt toys
201. Take out favor boxes
202. Shaped confetti
203. Halloween monster wreath
204. Saint Patrick's Day four-leafed clovers
205. Monogrammed Christmas bulbs
206. Lesson plan binder
207. Recipe cards
208. Giant Scrabble tiles
209. Scrapbook layouts
210. Dress-up trunk
211. History diorama
212. Pinewood derby car
213. Marshmallow slingshot
214. Themed cupcake liners
215. Princess party favors
216. Autumn leaf décor
217. Metal etchings
218. Paper quill pens
219. Decorative crystals
220. Party invitations
221. Cookie boxes
222. Doll clothes
223. Buffet dish labels

224. Advanced paper airplanes
225. Ship in a bottle
226. Hand bound sketchbook
227. Name tags
228. Infinity scarf
229. Magnetic bookmark
230. Chore chart
231. Meal planning notebook
232. Bingo boards
233. School folders
234. Science fair board
235. Lamp shades
236. Tissue paper tiki torches
237. Jack O' Lantern templates
238. Craft kit gifts
239. Piñata
240. Multi-pocket pencil case
241. Family photo album
242. Paper cranes
243. Easter egg tree
244. Play swords
245. Cardboard fort
246. Scrapbook pages
247. Leather pyramid purse

248. Caterpillar pencil pouch
249. Workbooks
250. Classroom activities
251. Birthday crown
252. Faux fur pocketbook
253. Paper dolls
254. Costume glasses
255. Superhero cape
256. Felted animals
257. Leather pet collar
258. Swatch card
259. Artist trading cards
260. Educational poster
261. Clock face
262. Inspiration board
263. Badges/buttons
264. Tissue paper ghosts
265. Wooden utensils
266. Pen wraps
267. Phone charger covers
268. Assignment book
269. Desktop calendar
270. Tablet case
271. Outdoor banner

272. Yard sale sign
273. Wooden marketplace sign
274. Reading chart
275. Bird whistle
276. Paper lei
277. Map poster
278. Scratch off cards
279. Faux stained glass window clings
280. Comic book pages
281. Book covers
282. Etched wood picture frame
283. Aged chalkboard sign
284. Chipboard bookends
285. Etched ceramic tea set
286. Dry erase wall
287. Drawer dividers
288. Toy car race track
289. Party drink dispensers
290. Shaped wood cutting board
291. State string art
292. Road trip planner
293. Potato stamps
294. Giant paper butterflies
295. Award medals

296. Marble tracks

297. Suede makeup bag

298. Faux leather passport cover

299. Monitor border

300. Snake necklace

301. Play wizard wands

302. Phone wrap sticker

303. Bedside organizer

304. Marble coasters

305. Mosaic vase

306. Bejeweled heart keychain

307. Woven leather ring

308. Envelope clutch

309. Fuzzy winter socks

310. Bubble cups

311. Lace table runner

312. Hamster/guinea pig/mouse toys

313. Shaped toss pillows

314. Confetti scrunchies

315. Book club mugs

316. Dream journal

317. File folder labels

318. Custom salt cellar

319. Flowery play tea set

320. Bug net
321. Document pouch
322. First aid kit
323. Embroidered handkerchief
324. Pool rules sign
325. Swirled ear cuff
326. Fish tank decorations
327. Scavenger hunt
328. Shot glass party favors
329. Keepsake glass box
330. Lace gloves
331. Display cabinet
332. Food labels
333. Garden markers
334. Bible case
335. Lettering practice sheet
336. Wall mural stencils
337. Paper doilies
338. Graffiti banner
339. Freezer organizers
340. Pet food bin
341. Snowflake garland
342. Rosebud headband
343. Custom hair clips

344. Christmas tree topper
345. Felt shamrocks
346. Birdhouse
347. Weather board
348. Braided rug
349. Ragdoll
350. Collage photo frame
351. Chocolate wrappers
352. Fanny pack
353. Embroidered calendar
354. Cosplay armor
355. Pin display
356. Baby blanket
357. Coffee tin
358. Award certificate
359. Paper party straws
360. Fill-in-the-blank games
361. Marker stand
362. Flower fairy lights
363. Antiqued cake stand
364. Drawstring backpack
365. Art portfolio
366. Weekly menu board
367. Sports team water bottles

368. Raffle tickets

369. Teabox

370. Wallpaper decal

371. Custom postage stamps

372. Shaped mousepad

373. Pizza slice holders

374. Invoices

375. Glitter containers

376. Dollhouse furniture

377. Custom paint palette

378. Cloth patches

379. Acrylic stamp

380. Resin rings

381. Crystal ball

382. Fortune cookie fortunes

383. Address book

384. Marathon runner numbers

385. Class election posters

386. Succulent centerpieces

387. Window herb garden

388. Fish mask

389. Pool diving toys

390. Soap dish

391. Etched serving bowl

392. Dog leash charms

393. Wooden monogram decoration

394. Reminder magnets

395. Information pamphlets

396. Pen pal envelopes

397. Custom baseball cards

398. Bookshelf labels

399. Mystery box

400. Sequined necklace

401. Game board

402. Dry erase plant pots

403. Monogrammed cigar box

404. Cat/dog toy box

405. Game cartridge storage

406. Progress poster

407. Motivational gym bag

408. Medication chart

409. Allergen bracelet

410. Baby book

411. Glasses holder necklace

412. Beaded edge blanket

413. Temperature record scarf

414. Personalized watch band

415. Health log

416. Lesson plans
417. Paper grass
418. Etched border mirror
419. DVD/game disc storage
420. Connect the dot games
421. Star chart
422. Witch's cauldron mug
423. Unicorn acrylic necklace
424. Plastic bugs
425. Refrigerator poetry magnets
426. Flowered flip flops
427. Non-slip coasters
428. Celestial hair pins
429. Birthstone brooch
430. Custom buttons
431. Tin punch signs
432. Washi tape holder
433. Dinosaur toothbrush holder
434. Handprint vase
435. Sewing patterns
436. Mail organizer
437. Felt play sets
438. Etched wedding champagne flutes
439. Alien costume

440. Spray painted sign
441. Tie-dye shirt with cutout design
442. Spooky eye Halloween window clings
443. Iced tea pitcher
444. Lemonade stand sign
445. Floating foam bath toys
446. Glass soap/lotion dispensers
447. Leather coin purse
448. Health and safety sign
449. Patterned pajama pants
450. Hand sewn moccasins
451. Ceiling light pull chain
452. Paper dragon
453. Bumblebee costume wings
454. Drink recipe tumbler
455. Burlap sack
456. Woven storage basket
457. Glitter star confetti
458. Balsa wood cake topper
459. Striped popcorn bucket
460. Framed calligraphy quotes
461. Purse organizer with pockets
462. Manicure templates
463. Recipe printed cookie tin

464. Decorated fruit bowl
465. Felt costume hats
466. Building brick toy storage
467. Play kitchen set
468. Mug cake recipe printed mug
469. Etched mason jar drinking glasses
470. Birthday signs
471. Dog shirts
472. Play ninja stars
473. Holographic pinwheels
474. Glitter bumper sticker
475. Key tags
476. Lottery games
477. Paper quilling art
478. Cleaning supply storage
479. Embossed leather band
480. Velvety slippers
481. Dog booties
482. Baby month onesies
483. Matching shampoo/conditioner/body wash containers
484. Potpourri sachets
485. Closet deodorizers
486. Thanksgiving cornucopia decorations
487. Pop culture-based props

488. Labels for homemade cosmetics

489. Recycled paper garlands

490. Family values wood sign

491. Custom tablecloth

492. Embossed holiday cards

493. Cardboard cutouts

494. Novelty sunglasses

495. Etched inkwell

496. Tiled wall clock

497. Desk catch-all

498. Mug sweater

499. 3D chipboard puzzles

500. Origami vase

Chapter 2: Some Project Ideas to Try and Get Practice

Design Your T-shirt

To make custom t-shirts using your Cricut machine, you will need to use iron-on or heat transfer vinyl. Ensure that you choose a color that contrasts and matches well with your t-shirt.

Materials

- Cricut Machine
- T-shirt
- Iron-on or heat transfer vinyl
- Fine point blade and light grip mat
- Weeding tools
- EasyPress (regular household iron works fine too, with a little extra work)
- Small towel and Parchment paper

Instructions

1. In preparing for this project, Cricut recommends that you prewash the cloth without using any fabric softener before applying the iron-on or heat transfer vinyl on it. Ensure that your T-shirt is dry and ready before you proceed.
2. On Cricut Design Space, create your design or import your SVG as described in the section on importing images.

3. If you are using an SVG file, select it and click on "Insert Images." When you do this, the image will appear in the Design Space canvas area.
4. Then, you need to resize the image to fit the T-shirt. To do this, select all the elements, then set the height and width in the edit panel area, or simply drag the handle on the lower right corner of the selection.
5. After this is done, select all the layers and click "Attach" at the bottom of the "Layers" panel, so that the machine cuts everything just as it is displayed on the canvas area.
6. You can preview your design using Design Space's templates. You access this by clicking the icon called "templates" on the left panel of Design Space's canvas. There, you can choose the surface on which to visualize your design. Choose the color of your vinyl and of the T-shirt so you can see how it will look once completed.
7. Once you are satisfied with the appearance of your design, click "Make It." If you have not connected your machine, you will be prompted to do so.
8. When the "Prepare" page shows, there is a "Mirror" option on the left panel. Ensure that you turn this on. This will make the machine cut it in reverse, as the top is the part that goes on to the T-shirt. Click "Continue."

9. Next, you are going to select the material. When using the Cricut Maker, you will do this in Cricut Design Space. Choose "Everyday Iron-On." On Cricut Explore Air, you select the material using the smart set dial on the machine. Set this dial to "Iron-On."
10. Now, it's time to cut. To cut vinyl (and other such light materials), you should use the light-grip blue mat. Place the iron-on vinyl on the mat with the dull side facing up. Ensure that there are no bubbles on the vinyl; you can do this using the scraper.
11. Install the fine point blade in the Cricut machine, then load the mat with the vinyl on it by tapping the small arrow on the machine. Then, press the "make it" button. When the machine is done cutting the vinyl, Cricut Design Space will notify you. When this happens, unload the mat.
12. With the cutting is done, it is time to weed. This must be done patiently so that you do not cut out the wrong parts. Therefore, you should have the design open as a guide.
13. After weeding, it is finally time to transfer the vinyl to the T-shirt. Before this, ensure that you have prewashed the T-shirt without fabric softener, as mentioned at the beginning of this project.
14. To transfer the design, you can use the EasyPress or a regular pressing iron. Using a pressing iron may be a little

more difficult, but it is certainly doable. Before you transfer, ensure that you have the EasyPress mat or a towel behind the material onto which you want to transfer the design so as to allow the material to be pressed harder against the heat.

15. Set the EasyPress to the temperature recommended on the Cricut heat guide for your chosen heat-transfer material and base material. For a combination of iron-on vinyl and cotton, the temperature should be set to 330 °F. After preheating the EasyPress, get rid of wrinkles on the T-shirt and press the EasyPress on it for about 5 seconds. Then, place the design on the T-shirt and apply pressure for 30 seconds. After this, apply the EasyPress on the back of the T-shirt for about 15 seconds.

16. If you're using a pressing iron, the process is similar; only that you need to preheat the iron to max heat and place a thin cloth on the design so that the iron does not have direct contact with the design or the T-shirt. This will prevent you from burning the T-shirt.

17. Wait for the design to cool off a bit, then peel it off while it is still a little warm.

18. Ensure that you wait for at least 24 hours after this before washing the T-shirt. When you do wash it, be sure to dry it inside out. Also, do not bleach the T-shirt.

Recipes Stickers

Materials

- "Cricut Maker" or "Cricut Explore"
- Sticker paper and cutting mat

Instructions

Step 1

Log in to the "Design Space" application and click on the "New Project" button on the top right corner of the screen to view a blank canvas.

Step 2

Click on the "Images" icon on the "Design Panel" and type in "stickers" in the search bar. Click on the desired image, and then click on the "Insert Images" button at the bottom of the screen.

Step 3

The selected image will be displayed on the canvas and can be edited using applicable tools from the "Edit Image Bar." You can make multiple changes to the image as you need, for example, you could change the color of the image or change its size (sticker should be between 2–4 inches wide). The image selected for this project has the words "stickers" inside the design, so let's delete that by first clicking on the "Ungroup" button and selecting the "Stickers" layer and clicking on the red "x" button. Click on the "Text" button and type in the name of your recipe, as shown in the picture below.

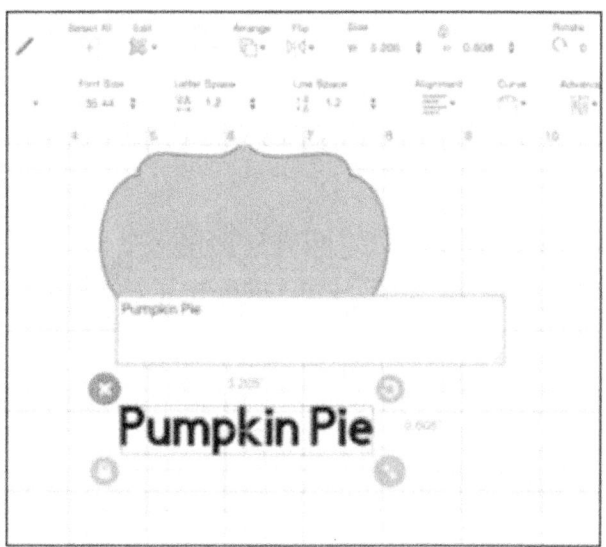

Step 4

Drag and drop the text in the middle of the design and select the entire design. Now, click on "Align" and select "Center Horizontally" and "Center Vertically."

Step 5

Select the entire design and click on the "Group" icon on the top right of the screen under "Layers panel." Now, copy and paste the designs and update the text for all your recipes.

Tip: Use your keyboard shortcut "Ctrl + C" and "Ctrl + V" to copy and paste the design.

Step 6

Click on "Save" at the top right corner of the screen to name and save your project.

Step 7

To cut your design, just click on the "Make It" button on the right corner of the screen. Load the sticker paper to your "Cricut" machine and click "Continue" at the bottom right corner of the screen to start cutting your design.

Note: The "Continue" button will only appear after you have purchased images and fonts that are only available for purchase.

Step 8

Set your cut setting to "Vinyl" (recommended for sticker paper since it tends to be thicker than regular paper). Place the sticker paper on top of the cutting mat and follow the prompts on the screen to finish cutting your design. Voilà! You have your own customized recipe stickers.

Floral Gold Flowerpot

This elegant gold and floral pot is the perfect finishing touch for any plant.

Description

This project makes a vinyl image for a metal flower pot.

Finished Size

Image is approximately 3.5" x 3.5" (9 cm x 9 cm)

Materials to Cut

- Premium Vinyl Patterned Sampler, Camilla

Everything Else

- StandardGrip Machine Mat—12" x 12"
- StandardGrip Vinyl Transfer Tape—12" x 48"
- Weeder
- Scraper
- Gold Metal Flowerpot

Preparation

If you'd like to change the layout, click Modify, then use Modify row tools to make adjustments before you slice.

Cut

Following Design Space's instructions to slice the vinyl photos.

Assemble

1. Utilize Weeder techniques to cut unnecessary parts. When weeding, it is usually cheaper to shift from inside out.

2. To apply the vinyl cuts to your project, use Transfer Tape and your Scraper Tool. Please ensure the areas on which you intend to stick are completely dry.

Wedding Invitation

Materials

- "Cricut Maker" or "Cricut Explore"
- Cutting mat and Cardstock or your choice of decorative paper/ crepe paper/ fabric
- Home printer (if not using "Cricut Maker")

Step 1

Log in to the "Design Space" application and click on the "New Project" button on the top right corner of the screen to view a blank canvas.

Step 2

Let's customize an already existing project by clicking on the "Projects" icon on the "Design Panel" and selecting "Cards" from the "All Categories" drop-down menu then type in "wedding invite" in the search bar.

Step 3

For example, you could select the project shown in the picture below and click "Customize" at the bottom of the screen to edit and personalize the text of your invite.

Step 4

Click "Text" on the "Designs Panel" and type in the details of the invite. You can change the font, color, and alignment of the text from the "Edit Text Bar" on top of the screen and remember to change the "Fill" to "Print" on the top of the screen.

Step 5

Select all the elements of the design and click on the "Group" icon on the top right corner of the screen under "Layers panel." Then, click on "Save" to save your project.

Step 6

Your design can now be printed and cut. Click on the "Make It" button and follow the prompts on the screen first to cut the printed design.

Designing a Card

One of the simplest projects to start with is a greeting card. You can use this process to make any type of greeting card you need to make. You can make birthday cards, sympathy cards, milestone cards, and so on.

For this project, we are going to make a birthday card. If you have a milestone birthday coming up, then your Cricut is going to serve you well.

Project Tools, Materials, and Accessories

1. Textured cardstock—light olive-green (or color of your choice)
2. Glossy or glitter cardstock—navy blue (or color of your choice)

3. Green Standard Grip Cricut mat
4. Cricut Fine-Point Blade
5. Scoring stylus
6. Cricut spatula
7. Pair of scissors for cutting the material to size
8. Glue

Instructions

1. Login in to Design Space and choose 'New Project.'
2. Once you have logged into Design Space, you will need to choose 'Images' from the bar on the left-hand side of the screen.
3. When you are on the 'Images' screen, you will need to choose 'Cartridges' from the top menu.
4. As you will be making a simple card, in the 'Search in cartridges' box, type in 'simple cards' in the search bar. Click the magnifying search button to begin the search.
5. There are 50 images, but only a few will appear on the screen. Click on the 'View all 50 images' button next to the box.
6. Scroll through the images until you find the card that says "Happy Birthday to You." Select the card and insert the image.

7. You will find that this birthday card comes with an envelope design. Highlight the envelope and hide it.
8. Change the size of the card so that it fits into a standard-sized envelope you can get at the store. Change the width to 10" and the height to 7".
9. Now is a good time to save the project. Choose a name you will recognize as you may want to use this project at a later stage. You should remember to save at important stages of the project as you progress through it.
10. Be careful with the stock board when you position it at the top of the mat. It has a tendency to peel back a bit when the Cricut starts to cut. Position the card mid-way to the bottom of the mat in Design Space.
11. When you put the actual cardstock onto the mat, you must put it with the textured side down. There will be a written message on the inside, which will be the smooth side.
12. In Design Space where you are setting the design, click mirror to flip the card correctly.
13. Select a font you like and type "Happy Birthday" positioned in the center of the card on the right-hand side.
14. You will need to choose 'Score' to get a line down the center where you will be folding the card. You do not need to use this, but it is handy. You can just as easily fold the card by hand if you do not have the scoring stylus.

15. After you click continue, the next step is to set up the material.
16. As the pattern is quite intricate, use the 'Cardstock' (for intricate cuts). Check your dial to make sure it is set correctly (use the custom setting).
17. Load the scoring stylus and the fine-point blade. Make sure they are loaded in the Cricut and selected in Design Space.
18. Place the olive-green cardstock on the mat with the rough side down.
19. Position it in the Cricut.
20. Load the mat into the Cricut and press the 'Load/Unload' button.
21. Press the 'Go' button when you are ready, and let the machine cut out the card.
22. Once the card has been cut, peel the mat away from the card. Use the spatula to carefully peel the card away, trying not to break the fine cut of the card.
23. Use two-sided tape or glue around the inside of the front of the card.
24. Cut the navy blue glossy or glitter cardstock to match the size of the card. Make it a tiny bit smaller.
25. Glue it or stick it down onto the card.
26. Your card is now ready to use.

Custom Notebooks

Materials

- "Cricut Maker" or "Cricut Explore"
- Cutting mat
- Washi sheets or your choice of decorative paper/ crepe paper/ fabric

Instructions

Step 1

Log in to the "Design Space" application and click on the "New Project" button on the top right corner of the screen to view a blank canvas.

Step 2

Use an already existing project from the "Cricut" library and customize it. So click on the "Projects" icon on the "Design Panel" and type in "notebook" in the search bar.

Step 3

Click on "Customize" so you can further edit the project to your preference. For example, the "unicorn notebook" project shown below. You can click on the "Linetype Swatch" to change the color of the design.

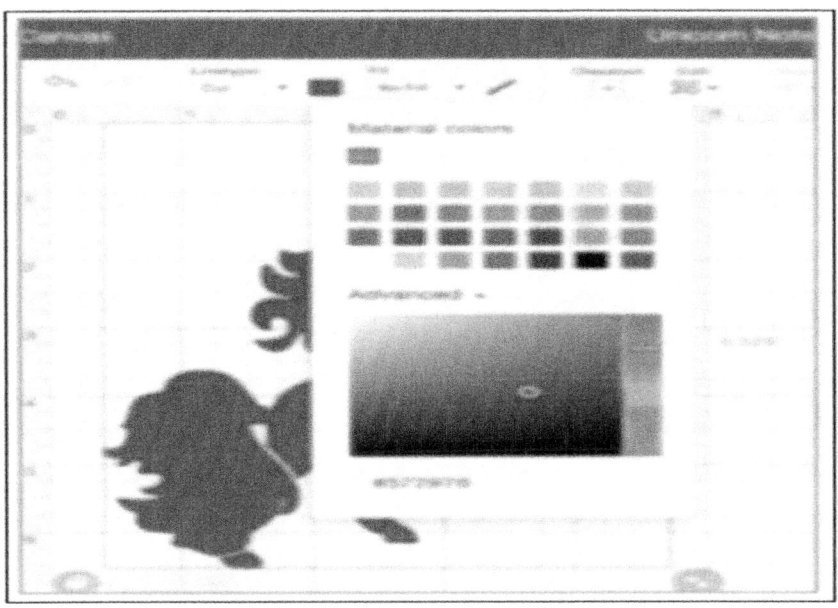

Step 4

The design is ready to be cut. Simply click on the "Make It" button and load the washi paper sheet to your "Cricut" machine and follow the instructions on the screen to cut your project.

Decorate You Mug

Materials

- "Cricut Maker" or "Cricut Explore"
- Standard grip mat
- Printable "Cricut" iron-on or heat transfer vinyl
- "Cricut EasyPress Mini"
- "EasyPress" mat
- Weeding tool
- Ceramic mug

Step 1

Log in to the "Design Space" application and click on the "New Project" button on the top right corner of the screen to view a blank canvas.

Step 2

Click on the "Images" icon on the "Design Panel" and type in "America" in the search bar. Click on the desired image, then click on the "Insert Images" button at the bottom of the screen.

Step 3

Click on the "Templates" icon on the "Designs Panel" on the left of the screen and type in "mug" in the templates search bar and select the mug icon.

Step 4

You can change the "Type" and "Size" of the template to decorate mugs with non-standard sizes by clicking on the "Size" icon and selecting "Custom" to update your mug size.

Step 5

You can further edit your design by clicking on the "Shapes" icon adding hearts, stars, or other desired shapes to your design.

Step 6

Click on "Save" at the top right corner of the screen and give the desired name to the project, for example, "Mug Decoration" and click "Save."

Step 7

The design is ready to be printed and cut. Simply click on the "Make It" button and follow the prompts on the screen for using an ink jet printer to print the design on your printable iron-on vinyl and subsequently cut the design.

Note: "One side of the Printable Iron-on Dark sheet is white with a matte finish; the other side is printed with blue grid lines. Print on the matte side; the side with the blue gridlines is the iron-on backing that will be removed before applying your design to your material."

Step 8

Carefully remove the excess material from the sheet using the "weeder tool," making sure only the design remains on the clear liner.

Step 9

Using the "Cricut EasyPress Mini" and "Easy Press Mat" the iron-on layers can be easily transferred to your mug. Preheat your "Easy Press Mini" and put your design on the desired area and apply pressure for a couple of minutes or more (sample project in the picture below). Wait for few minutes before peeling off the design while it is still warm. (Since the design is delicate, use the spatula tool or your fingers to rub the letters down the mug before starting to peel the design.)

Paper Flowers

Materials

- "Cricut Maker" or "Cricut Explore"
- Cutting Mat
- Cardstock
- Adhesive

Instructions

Step 1

Log in to the "Design Space" application and click on the "New Project" button on the top right corner of the screen to view a blank canvas.

Step 2

Click on the "Images" icon on the "Design Panel" and type in "flower" in the search bar. Click on the desired image, then click on the "Insert Images" button at the bottom of the screen.

Step 3

The selected image will be displayed on the canvas and can be edited using applicable tools from the "Edit Image Bar." Then copy and paste the flower five times and make them a size smaller than the preceding flower to create a variable size for depth and texture for the design, as shown in the picture below.

Step 4

The design is ready to be cut. Simply click on the "Make It" button and load the cardstock to your Cricut machine and follow the instructions on the screen to cut your project.

Step 5

Once the design has been cut, simply remove the cut flowers and bend them at the center. Then, using the adhesive, stack flowers with the largest flowers at the bottom.

Make Your Own Doormat

Materials

- Cricut machine
- Scrap cardstock (the color does not matter)
- Coir mat (18" x 30")
- Outdoor acrylic paint
- Vinyl stencil
- Transfer tape
- Flat round paintbrush
- Cutting mat (12" x 24")

Instructions

1. Create your design in Cricut Design Space. You can also download an SVG design of your choice and import it into Cricut Design Space. Make sure that your design is the right size; resize it to ensure.

2. Cut the stencil. You do this by clicking "Make it" in Cricut Design Space when you are done with the design. After this, you select "Cardstock" as the material. Then, you press the "Cut" button on the Cricut machine.

3. When this is done, remove the stencil from the machine and weed.

4. On the reverse side of the stencil, apply spray glue. After this, attach the stencil to the doormat, exactly where you want your design to be; then, pick up the letter bits left on the cutting mat and glue them to their places in the stencil on the doormat.

5. The following step is to mask the parts of the doormat that you don't want to paint on. You can do this using painters' plastic.

6. Now, it's time to spray-paint your stencil on the doormat. Keeping the paint can about 5 inches away from the doormat, spray up and down, keeping the can pointed

straight through the stencil. If it is at an angle, the paint will get under the stencil and ruin your design. Spray the entire stencil 2–3 times to make sure that you do not miss any part and that the paint is even.

7. You're just about done! Now, remove the masking plastic and the stencil and leave the doormat for about one hour to get dry.

Leaf Banner

Materials

- "Cricut Maker" or "Cricut Explore"
- Standard grip mat
- Watercolor paper and paint
- Felt balls
- Needle and thread
- Hot glue

Instructions

Step 1

Log in to the "Design Space" application and click on the "New Project" button on the top right corner of the screen to view a blank canvas.

Step 2

Let's use an already existing project from the Cricut library and customize it. So click on the "Projects" icon and type in "leaf banner" in the search bar.

Step 3

Click on "Customize" so you can further edit the project to your preference or simply click on the "Make It" button and load the watercolor paper to your Cricut machine and follow the instructions on the screen to cut your project.

Step 4

Use watercolors to paint the leaves and let them dry completely. Then create a garland using the needle and thread through the felt balls and sticking the leaves to the garland with hot glue.

Make a 3D Paper Flower

Materials

- Cricut machine
- Cricut mat
- Colored scrapbook paper
- Hot glue gun and glue sticks

Where to Find Materials

- Express vinyl
- Craft stash
- Happy crafter
- Amazon
- Etsy
- Cricut.com
- Swing design

Instructions

1. To make flowers, you need an appropriate shape for the petals. To make such a shape, you can combine three ovals of equal size. To create an oval, select the circle tool, then

create a circle. Then click the unlock button at the bottom of the shape. Once this is done, you can reshape the circle to form an oval.

2. Duplicate this oval twice and rotate each duplicate a little, keeping the bottom at the same point, as shown in the picture.

3. Select all three ovals and weld them together to get your custom petal shape. For each large flower, you need 12 petals—each one about 3 inches long, while for each small flower, you need 8 petals—each one about 2 inches long. For each flower, you also need a circle shape for the base of about the same width as each petal. Arrange the petals and base circle shape in Cricut Design Studio.

4. After you cut out the petals, remove them and cut a slit about half an inch long in the bottom of each one. Place a bit of glue on the left side and glue the right side over the glue for each petal.

5. The next thing to do is to place the petals on the circle base. For large flowers, you need three circles of four petals each. For small flowers, you need five circles on the outside and three on the inside. Put a bit of hot glue on the petal and add to the circle as described above.

6. For the center of the flowers, search Cricut Access for "flower" and chose shapes with several small petals. Cut

these out using a different color of cardstock and glue to the center of the flowers.

Tip and Tricks

If you do not have a spatula or scrappers to get things off your mat, you can use a two-inch putty knife to get things off your mat.

Painter's tape can be used as a transfer tape on the fly and it has sixty yards in some cases.

If you have smaller transfers, scotch tape works in a pinch as well.

Double-sided tape can help keep the corners down on your mat that has lost stick in spots. Scotch brand makes a removable one that is small and sturdy.

Paper Luminary

Materials

- "Cricut Maker" or "Cricut Explore"
- Standard grip mat
- Shimmer paper sampler
- Weeder
- Spray adhesive
- Frosted glass luminary

Instructions

Step 1

Log in to the "Design Space" application and click on the "New Project" button on the top right corner of the screen to view a blank canvas.

Step 2

Let's use an already existing project from the Cricut library and customize it. So click on the "Projects" icon and type in "paper luminary" in the search bar.

Step 3

Click on "Customize" to further edit the project to your preference or simply click on the "Make It" button and load the shimmer paper to your Cricut machine and follow the instructions on the screen to cut your project.

Step 4

Cut and weed the design, then spray the back of the shimmer paper with spray adhesive and adhere to the glass luminary, as shown in the picture below.

Adorn Your Pillow or Cushion

Materials

- Black, dark blue, or dark purple fabric
- Heat-transfer vinyl in gold or silver
- Cutting mat
- Polyester batting
- Weeding tool or pick
- Cricut EasyPress

Instructions

1. Decide the shape you want for your pillow and cut two matching shapes out of the fabric.

2. Open Cricut Design Space and create a new project.
3. Select the "Image" button in the lower left-hand corner and search for stars.
4. Select the stars of your choice and click "Insert."
5. Place the iron-on material on the mat.
6. Send the design to the Cricut.
7. Use the weeding tool or pick to remove excess material.
8. Remove the material from the mat.
9. Place the iron-on material on the fabric.
10. Use the EasyPress to adhere it to the iron-on material.
11. Sew the two fabric pieces together, leaving a seam allowance and a small space open.
12. Fill the pillow with polyester batting through the small open space.
13. Sew the pillow shut.
14. Cuddle up to your starry pillow!

Chapter 3: Tips and Tricks for Project Ideas

Wood

The wood projects tend to be time-consuming and labor-intensive and, of course, long-lasting. So you want to get it right the first time. Below are some tips to help you get the best wood projects with no stress:

- Ensure that your projects are carried out using a sealer so that the wood does not get damaged unexpectedly.

- When using vinyl or iron-on designs, use sanding paper to sand the wood and obtain a flat surface before the application of the design. Wooden plaques are not always flat, as it's a natural product. The surface may need to be sanded so that all sections of the design material will stick evenly on the surface.

- Consider using a stamping effect for your paper design when using wood and paper designs to produce a rustic feel for your project.

- When choosing a stain color for the wooden plaque, make sure that your project color aligns with that color and other projects that you already have in your house. Don't be scared to combine different wood stain colors and use your own customized stain!

- For easy and effective application of wood glue, it is recommended to wet the wood with a damp cloth first. After the wood glue has been applied to the plaque, clamp it, and allow it to set for at least 24 hours.

- If you are planning to use pallet wood, make sure to clean the pallet plaque using a wire brush.

Iron-on

It is important to remember that you put the liner side of the iron-on sheet facing down on the cutting mat and mirror the design by clicking on the "Mirror" button below the cutting mat before cutting the design. You can also adjust the settings of your Cricut machine to obtain a "kiss-cut," which only cuts through the iron-on film and leaves the liner intact. For example, if you are using Cricut Maker, use the "premium fine point blade" and select "Browse all materials," then select "Everyday Iron-on." For Cricut Explore lines, turn the smart set dial to "Custom" and select "Everyday Iron-on" and again using the "premium fine point blade." Now, here are some tips on the application of "Everyday Iron-on":

- Make sure the clothing item you are going to apply to your design is clean and pre-washed. Prewashing will help remove any chemical-based colors from the garment and eliminate any shrinking that might occur after the first wash.

- Remember to pre-heat, heat, and post-heat the design on the garment for a recommended amount of time to ensure the design is set into the fibers of the garment.

- Do not apply any kind of iron-on material on top of a glitter iron-on design, since any other layer over the glitter layer will start to peel away upon washing.

- For household iron, use the "Cotton/Linen" setting, which is usually the highest temperature, setting for the iron.

- If using a steam iron, turn off the steam before application.

- Pre-heat the area of the garment for 10–15 seconds before putting your design on it.

- Avoid using a flimsy ironing board and instead, use a firm and flat surface around waist high.

- Use a press cloth or a dishtowel over the liner side of the material to protect it from the direct heat of the iron.

- In case a portion of the design is not sticking, then replace the liner over the film and iron the portion again for 10 seconds with firm pressure.

- For any embellished items, do not wash them for at least 24 hours after the application of the iron-on design and always wash these garments inside out.

- Do not layer the glitter iron-on on top of "Holographic Sparkle, Holographic, Foil, Glitter Mesh, Glitter, or flocked iron-on."

- Iron-on designs are recommended to be used with 100% cotton, 100% polyester, and poly/cotton blends.

- Pre-heat the clothing item for 10 to 15 sec, then place the design onto the pre-heated area. Heat each portion of the design for 50 seconds with medium pressure, then flip the garment and heat the backside of the design for 15 seconds. Once the design has been completely cooled, remove the lining.

Vinyl

Using Vinyl, you can earn a lot of money in so many ways. Here are some tips to make your life easier:

- Use Cricut Premium Vinyl for projects that may end up enduring harsh weather like mugs, outdoor signs, mailboxes, and more, since it is water-resistant as well as UV resistant with an adhesive that can last for up to 3 years.

- Due to the strong adhesive that underlines the Cricut Premium Vinyl, once the design has been positioned on the base material, it is hard to reposition the design without causing any damage.

- Use Cricut Premium Vinyl, removable for projects that you may want to alter after a certain period of time, or maybe you are looking to change things up every now and then when it comes to your home décor. This removable vinyl stays removable for up to 2 years and can be removed without leaving any residue behind.

- To remove the vinyl sheet from the cutting mat, instead of lifting the vinyl from the mat, peel the mat away for a smoother release of the design with no damage.

- If you are not using the "kiss-cut" and cutting through both the vinyl and the liner, then you can just peel away the liner from the vinyl and apply it to the desired surface with your hands and without the transfer tape.

- It is recommended to peel the liner at a 45-degree angle, and in the case that the vinyl does not detach from the liner, then simply polish the transfer tape on the vinyl and try to separate again.

Chapter 4: Other Projects

Leafy Garland

Garlands are an easy way to spruce up any space, and there is an infinite variety of them. Create a unique leafy one to give your home a more naturalistic feel! Feel free to change the colors of the leaves to suit you, whether you stick with green or go a little more unnatural. Tweaking the size of the bundles you make and how close you put them together will change the look of the garland. You can use different types of leaves as well. Experiment a little bit to see what you like best. Bending the leaves down the center and curling the edges a little will give you a more realistic look, or you can leave them flat for a handmade look. You can use Cricut Explore 1, Cricut Explore Air 2 or Cricut Maker for this project.

Materials

- Cardstock—2 or more colors of green, or white to paint yourself
- Glue gun
- Lightstick cutting mat
- Weeding tool or pick
- Floral wire
- Floral tape

Instructions

1. Select the "Image" button in the lower left-hand corner and search for "leaf collage."
2. Select the image of leaves and click "Insert."
3. Place your cardstock on the cutting mat.
4. Send the design to your Cricut.
5. Remove the outer edge of the paper, leaving the leaves on the mat.
6. Use a pick or scoring tool to score down the center of each leaf lightly.
7. Use your weeding tool or carefully pick to remove the leaves from the mat.

8. Gently bend each leaf at the scoreline.
9. Glue the leaves into bunches of two or three.
10. Cut a length of floral wire to your desired garland size, and wrap the ends with floral tape.
11. Attach the leaf bunches to the wire using floral tape.
12. Continue attaching leaves until you have a garland of the size you want. Bundle lots of leaves for a really full look, or spread them out to be sparser.
13. Create hooks at the ends of the garland with floral wire.
14. Hang your beautiful leaf garland wherever you'd like!

Box

Materials

- The Cricut machine
- Color papers
- Glue
- Removable golden vinyl
- Gold Marker
- The template
- The typos used are Courier new and Adalaide (the latter is from Cricut)

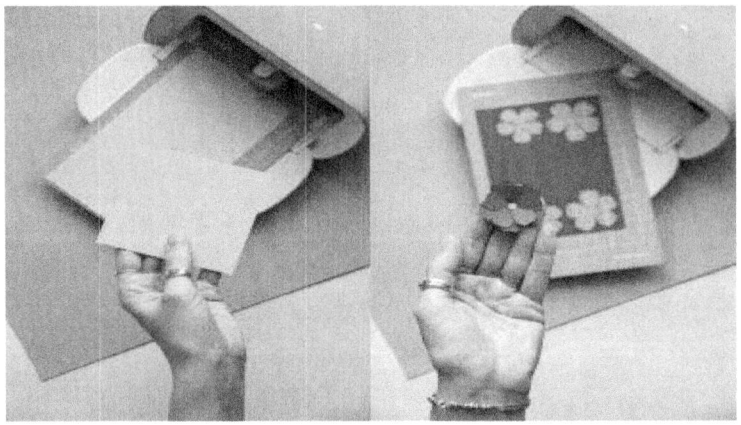

Instructions

1. Using your application prepare, the cutting of your paper templates for your box, as well as the paper decorations (ex: leaves/flowers/hearts).
2. Prepare the cutting of your heart stickers with your smart vinyl removable Gold paper that you will use to close your box.
3. Now that the paper templates are cut out, use your gold marker to create and draw your texts. You can choose to write whatever you want.

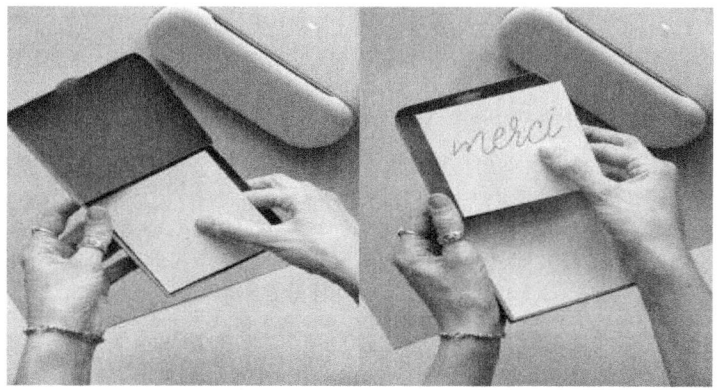

4. It's time to stick your papers on your cardboard box. The "Thank you" paper is to be placed inside the box on the upper part. Also, place your plain pink paper template at the bottom of your box.
5. Now stick your paper with your text "Just for you" on the outside of the box.

6. Come and create your floral arrangement inside your box using strong glue, I decided to add a real Craspedia to it so that I don't just have paper. If not, you can add a branch of eucalyptus or olive tree.

7. Once your interior decoration is finished, you can now close your box and seal it with your golden heart stickers. All you have to do is offer them.

Shamrock Earrings

Materials

- Cricut Maker
- Earring (from a Cricut Project)
- Rotary Wheel
- Knife Blade
- FabricGrip Mat
- StrongGrip Mat
- Weeder Tool
- Cricut Leather
- Scraper Tool
- Adhesive
- Pebbled-Faux Leather
- Earring Hooks

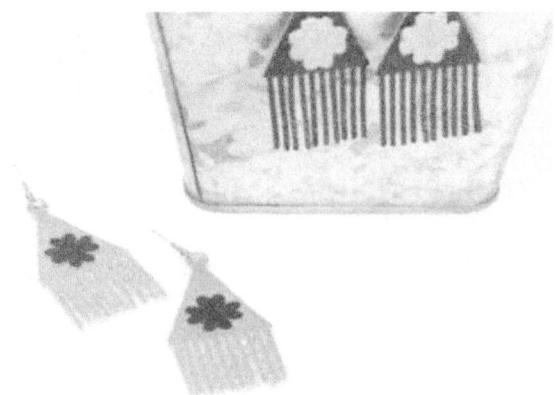

Instructions

1. First, open the Cricut Project (Earring). You can now either click on "Make It" or "Customize" to edit it.

2. Once you've selected one, click on "Continue."

3. Immediately the Cut page pops up, select your material and wait for the "Load" tools and Mat to appear.

4. Make your Knife blade your cutting tool in clamp B. This will be used on the Leather.

5. On the StrongGrip Mat, place the Leather and make sure it's facing down. Then load the Mat into the machine and tap the "Cut" flashing button.

6. When the scoring has been done, go back to the cutting tool and change it to Rotary Wheel so that you can use it on the Faux Leather.

7. Similarly, place your faux leather on your FabricGrip Mat, facing down. Then load the Mat into the machine and tap the "Cut" flashing button.

8. Take away all the items on the Mat with your Scraper tool. Be careful with the small fringes though.

9. Make a hole on the top circle by making use of the Weeder tool. Make sure the hole is large enough to make the Earring hooks fit in.

10. If necessary, you may have to twist the hook's end with the pliers to fit them in.

11. Close them up after you have looped them inside the hole that was made inside the Earring.

12. Finally, you should glue the Shamrock to the surface of the Earring with adhesive.

13. Wait for it to dry before using.

Handmade Flower Corsage

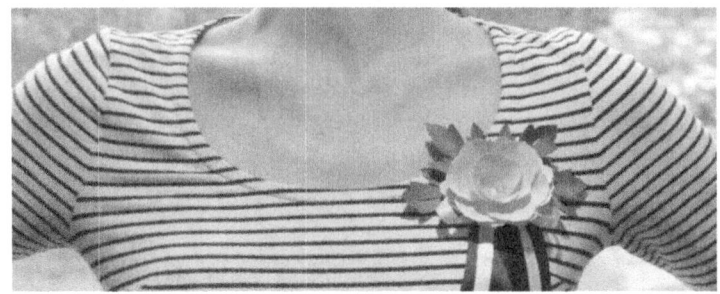

You are probably interested in making this year's Mother's Day extra special. I have been able to create this simply handmade flower corsage just in five easy steps. Furthermore, this paper corsage is also good for Prom, especially when you make it to match your Prom gown.

Materials

- Glue
- Scissors
- The cardstock (which would obviously be the choice for the flowers and the leaves)
- Ribbon or pins
- Templates

Instructions

1. There are some pre-installed designs, so you just get them and pint them on the color of your chosen card. The Cricut Explore would be used to cut it.

2. We would gently spray the paper with water. This would allow the paper to curl into that desired shape and make the paper form several shapes.

3. You make use of the glue to join those tabs together on each section and make sure it dries. I use a clothing pin so that it would stick together while it dries.

4. Make use of watercolors or makers to add colorful edges around before you glue all the petals and the leaves to form that flower and allow it to dry.

5. You may decide to make a wrist corsage. Doing this would require you to cut the desired ribbon length and then glue it with the finished flower. Simple. You may decide to use a pin on the back of the flower.

Felt Side Banner

Materials

- Dowel slice to 5.5"
- Felt
- Heated glue
- Yarn

Instructions

1. Plugin your heated glue firearm to get it warmed up; at that point, cut your felt utilizing the turning sharp edge and texture tangle. Strip away the additional felt. It resembles enchantment!

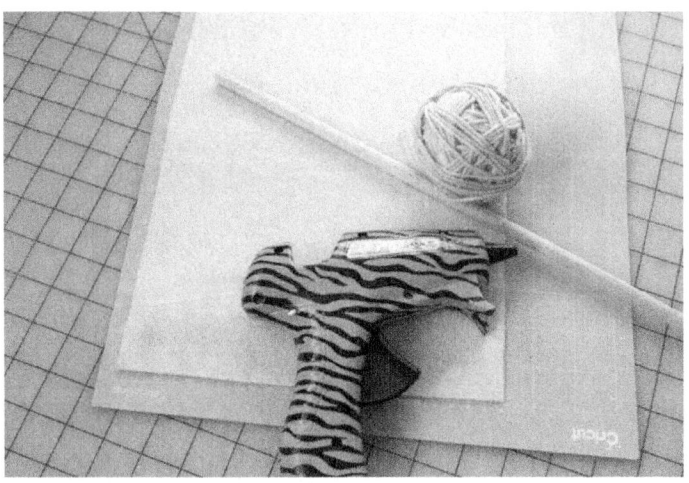

2. Strip off the flag. Spot the dowel on top and crease over the top edge to see where the dowel should be set.

3. Include a line of craft glue.

4. Carefully overlay the top over. On the off chance that you have a low-temp stick firearm or thick felt, you may have the option to squeeze it down with your fingers, yet to be protected, you could utilize a pencil or the rest of the dowel, so you don't consume your fingers.

Personalized Phone Cover

Using a protective case for your fun can also be a lot of fun—especially with the Cricut machine—you can change designs and refresh the style of your phone with each new phone case project you decide to make. And, you only need a few more things to start aside from your Cricut machine.

Materials

- Foil Adhesive Vinyl
- Transfer tape
- Clear phone case—more room for fun!
- Weeding tool
- Scissors or scalpel
- Cricut machine—Cricut Maker or Cricut Explore Air

Instructions

1. As always, when starting out fresh, click on "New Project" to open a blank canvas. You can make this project a breeze by clicking on "Templates." Here you can find templates for numerous different projects, which include phone cases as well. Choose the phone case template. Make sure to size the template layer to fit the size of the clear phone case you have prepared for the project. From there, you can start working on your design. You can add images of your choice and resize them as needed to make a phone case design. Once your design is ready to go, you will click "Select All" then choose the "Attach" option. This will prepare the design for cutting as you need both the phone case rectangle layer cut out and the designs used for the phone case.

2. If you are happy with your design you can click on "Make it." Before proceeding with cutting, choose Foil Adhesive Vinyl as your material. Set up the cutting mat and prepare the material to start cutting.

3. Now that your design is cut out, it's time to use the weeding tool. Remove all excess vinyl from the design—in this case, excess material would be the background while your designs (butterflies for example) should remain intact. Next, attach the transfer tape to the vinyl and remove the

backing paper. Attach the vinyl to the phone case with the transfer tape. You will use your scissors or a scalpel to remove the excess part of the vinyl once it is attached to the phone case—remove those parts that don't fit the phone case design. For instance, you will need to remove the part of the vinyl piece covering the camera slot on the phone case. Remove the tape, and voilà! You have your own personalized phone case. You can make as many designs as you like using these guidelines.

Paper Succulents in a Container

Project inspired by The Happy Scrap

This pretty little project can be made to fit into any container you already have and can instantly add a little punch to your mantelpiece, table setting, or display. Make as many or as few of these different succulents as you want.

Materials

- Cardstock in teals and pinks
- Ink pads in different coordinating colors of teal and pink
- Sponges or dabbers for the ink
- Hot glue gun

- Foam to fill your container

Instructions

Step 1

In Design Space, look for the design file for succulents. If you want to create the design yourself, create one large petal-shaped flower and then copy it about six times. Scale each copy down to a smaller size. If necessary, remove a petal or two to make it appear more proportional. For the spiral and pointed succulent, make a spiral with three rings. The center of the ring should be a circle at the end. Add pointed triangles to the outside of the spiral lines.

Step 2

Once you have your designs ready, send your file to cut on your different colored card stock. Remove your pieces and place corresponding flower pieces together on a covered work surface. Using your sponges or dabbers, add a touch of ink to the outer edges of each petal shape or on the tips of the spikes of the spiral. You can keep the colors matching or contrast with a pink tip on a teal succulent and vice versa.

Step 3

Gently curl the edges of the petals up at the ends to make them more three-dimensional.

Step 4

Using your hot glue gun, glue the layers of the succulents together and roll the pointed succulents and glue them together as well.

Step 5

Place the floral foam inside your container, about ½ inch from the top. You can place your succulents on the foam or glue them down in the place where you like the arrangement. Once all your succulents are placed, consider covering the exposed foam with paper grass or shredded paper. You can glue this covering down if you like, but it typically looks best when it is loose.

Creative Herbarium

Learn how to dry your plants recovered in nature and collect them in your herbarium notebook or draw them in small drawing notebooks made by yourself.

Materials

- Scandicraft Collection Herbarium Album
- Block of 24 assorted printed papers A4
- Assortment of 3 sheets of stickers
- Wooden press "My herbarium"
- Drawing pad A5 80 sheets—90g—Monali
- A4 paper cutter

- Cricut Maker
- Assortment of 3 washi tapes
- Fine black felt pen
- Double-sided adhesive tape—6mm x 10m
- Sewing needle
- Sewing thread
- 1 pair of scissors
- Downloadable envelope and notebook templates

Instructions

1. Use the press and the herbarium book 1. Collect fresh plants and flowers. Open the press to dry the plants. Take out the items: cardboard boxes, sheets of paper, and foam.

2. Place a sheet of thin paper on cardboard. Position the plant to dry. Cut back the stem if necessary. Cover with a second sheet of thin paper. In addition to this, you need to know more about it.

3. Stack the cardboard boards on top of each other. Place in the press. Cover the last plant with a thin sheet and cardboard. Add the mousses. In addition to this, you need to know more about it.

4. Close the press on the plants. Screw as far as possible to crush the plants. Leave to dry for at least a week, especially for plants that are thick.

5. Gently remove the plants and flowers from the press. Open the herbarium notebook. Place the flowers and plants in the chosen location. Maintain with a piece of washi tape from the collection. Stick the rose with double-sided adhesive tape. Write the names of the plants. Stick a label to date the harvest and create a paper envelope to insert petals, seeds, etc.

6. Choose a paper from the collection. Fold in half crosswise. Measure 10.5 cm at the fold and cut with Cricut. Take 4 sheets of drawing paper. Fold them in half and cut them in the same way as for the blanket.

7. Mark the points to be drilled at the fold of the sheets using the template to download in Cricut. Pierce the leaves at the marks. Cut a sewing thread folded in 3. Pass the needle from the inside of the booklet to the cover. Bring the needle back to the center of the notebook and tie it at the fold. Do the same for each pair of holes.

8. Cut the sheets that protrude from the notebook using the cutter. Decorate the cover with masking tape from the collection. Choose stickers and glue them in the center to

finish decorating the cover. In addition to this, you need to know more about it.

9. Your notebooks are ready to be filled with pretty dried plants or drawn during your walks.

Geometric Lampshade

Materials

- White cardstock
- Metallic cardstock if you prefer
- Ribbon or string
- Hot glue gun

Instructions

1. In Design Space, go into the library and enter the "Make It Now" unit. Find the project labeled "Geo Ball."
2. Once the project loads, place your cardstock on your cutting mat and send it to score the fold lines.

3. Once your paper is scored, glue the metallic and white pieces of paper together. Begin folding the paper to create the geometric shape. Place a line of glue along one edge and bring the project into its final shape.
4. If you are hanging your pendant, make sure to attach your ribbon or string to the bottom of the shape and hang it from your ceiling!

Takeout-Style Boxes

Materials

- Sticker paper for labels or stickers
- Cardstock

- Hot glue gun or glue dots

Instructions

1. If you are going to add labels of stickers to your boxes, design them in Design Space with the image or text that you prefer. Consider adding the title of the event and the date to the label so guests know right away how long they have the leftovers in their fridge. Create a variety of sizes so they will fit over the cardstock boxes you are about to create or other containers you might need to use.
2. Once your stickers or labels are created, send the file to print and cut.
3. Search in the Design Space library the template for Chinese Take Out Boxes and load it into a new workspace. Choose a variety of sizes. Load your cardstock onto your cutting mats and send the file to cut.
4. Fold your cut cardstock along the score lines. Apply glue along the edges to assemble the box and reinforce the seams.
5. If you are adding stickers to your boxes, add them now. For other containers, keep the stickers nearby or apply them onto them as well. You are ready to send your guests away in style now!

Cricut Foil Streamers

Materials

- Cricut party foil in colors of your choice
- Green StandardGrip mat
- Cricut Fine-Point Blade
- Weeding tool
- Scraper tool

Directions

1. Start a new project in Design Space.
2. Select 'Images' from the left-hand side menu.
3. Search for image #M7D2D9CA.
4. Choose 'Square' from the 'Shapes' menu on the left-hand side menu.
5. Click 'Make it.'

6. Position the spiral in the middle of the board to give the Cricut enough cutting room.
7. Cut the party foil to the size of the cutting mat and stick it onto the mat.
8. Use either the brayer or scraping tool to ensure the foil is smooth and stuck down properly to the mat.
9. Make sure the fine-point blade is loaded into the Cricut.
10. Load the cutting mat with the foil into the Cricut.
11. Set the Cricut dial to custom.
12. In Design Space, click 'Continue.'
13. Select 'Party foil' as the material.
14. Click 'Continue.'
15. When the Cricut is ready to cut, click 'Go.'
16. When the Cricut has finished cutting, unload the cutting mat.
17. Carefully remove the excess foil and use the weeding tool to weed the small starts on the foil.
18. Use the spatula to gently remove the streamer from the cutting mat.

Chapter 5: How to Make Your First Art Sale Online

Setting up a Website

This is a very important step in the right direction, and here's how you can go about it:

1. Choose a Domain Name/URL

This is very important because your audience or customers will know you, and everything you create and the post will be linked to this domain name. Usually, you can pick one that depicts your brand and what you do. It must be short and easy to remember too.

2. Register Your Domain Name/URL

This can be done with little cash, usually per annum, and it helps link your domain name to your hosting service. I would recommend using GoDaddy for domain and hosting services.

3. Choosing a Hosting Service

You will need a hosting service to host your website, and depending on their customer service, reliability, speed, storage space, among others, you can choose one that is very good.

4. Connect Your Domain Name to Your Web Host

Some web hosts will not need this step as they offer domain names with their hosting service. However, you will have to connect your domain name by plugging your server name/DNS into your domain name registrar account.

5. Install WordPress

WordPress is an application that allows you to manage and work on your website, and it is free, straightforward, and consumer-friendly.

6. Choose a Theme for Your Website

Get one that suits your brand, content, and services. You can get them free or subscribe to Premium ones at a price.

7. Configure Your Website

Now that you've got a functional website with a theme, you may want to configure your website. You will want to organize the information you give about what you do and what you have to offer, add one or more colors, and make it easy for visitors to navigate your site.

8. Add Content

Get all yourself out there by uploading, writing, and posting what you have to offer on your website. Something that will appeal to your customers and leave them satisfied.

If setting up your website is something you know you may not be able to do on your own, you can employ the service of a web developer to create your website. This will help you focus on making money with your Cricut by creating more designs.

Advertising

Common ways of advertising as a new service provider include:

- Social media ads on Instagram, Pinterest, Facebook, and other social media sites.
- Video Ads on blogs, YouTube, etc.
- Digital display ads
- Magazines and newspapers
- Direct mail and personal sales

Other means are:

- Outdoor Advertising

- Radio and Podcasts
- Product Placement on Television shows and YouTube channels
- Email marketing
- Event marketing

Taking Orders and Shipping

Customers can place orders via email or contact phone numbers that you place on your website. It could be daily or within specified time limits or days, depending on how well you can deliver. Ensure you get all necessary arrangements in place before taking orders from areas far from your reach to prevent disappointments and delays; thus, ruining your reputation as a service provider.

Shipping arrangements depend on your location and the taxes involved.

Saving Money Using Your Cricut Machine for Business

You can employ the services of any bank or saving institution around you to build your financial strength and grow your wealth.

Note:

1. If you took a loan, ensure you pay off your debt.

2. On your first batch of sales, take out your capital to continue business and save the profit.

Chapter 6: Troubleshooting

Optimizing Speed and Connection

Generally speaking, working with the Design Space software is pretty easy and free from glitches and problems. Of course, there is always room for improvement and errors that occur throughout the process, as is the case with anything technology-related, right? The most common complaints about the software system for Cricut is that it fails to open, freezes up, is slow to load, and crashes. To help you troubleshoot some of these common errors, follow the advice below.

The first thing you should check is your Internet connection. This is the primary cause of Design Space problems. You need a good upload and download speed consistently for the program to run smoothly.

Spikes and dips in your connection can make things glitch. If you can, try placing your router next to your machine so it can get a consistent connection.

Some websites and software only need a good download speed, but it does not depend on upload speed. This is not the case with Design Space. You need both for it to work well. This is because you are constantly uploading and downloading information into the system for your various projects. Having a good download speed is great, but if your upload speed is slow, you could experience some slow loading, etc.

To learn about your computer Internet speed, try running a test. There are various services out there like Ookla or speedtest.net that will help you learn more about your Internet speed. In order to properly test this, you will want to have a Bluetooth connection or a USB port open. Remember, the speeds you need, according to Cricut, are 1 or 2 Mbps for uploading and 2 or 3 Mbps for downloading. If you run a test and your numbers are lower than this, call up your Internet provider and ask for a new modem or router. It can be a pain waiting for it to arrive, but it can make a huge difference if your current one is just not cutting it.

Sometimes it is not a problem with your Internet. Sometimes it is a problem with your computer or the device from which you are trying to work in Design Space. Like your Internet speeds, Cricut has guidelines for optimal operations. Below is a breakdown of the primary requirements for different types of computers:

Apple Computers

- 1.83 GHz CPU

- 4GB Ram

- 50MB free space

- Bluetooth enabled or available USB port

- MAC OS X 10.12 or newer operating system

Windows Computers

- 4GB Ram

- 50MB free space

- Bluetooth enabled or open USB port

- AMD processor or Intel Core series

- Windows 8 or newer operating system

Sometimes all you need to do is clear up some space on your computer or update your operating system (happens automatically) to optimize Design Space on your device. Other times it is not really about the space or operating system on your computer, but it has to do with the other programs running in the background at the same time as Design Space. Anything that you have open while you are trying to use Design Space can cause a drain on the program. This is especially true if the other program is using your Internet to download or upload or stream information from the Internet. You may not need to close down all your open programs aside from Design Space, but try shutting a couple down that you think could be slowing you down.

In addition to the above general troubleshooting suggestions, here are a few more suggestions to help your general problems:

- Check malware and clean up as necessary
- Defrag your hard drive
- For Windows users, update your drivers
- Update antivirus software if necessary
- Clear out your history and cache (with ccleaner)

These can help your Internet speed but can also potentially solve your problems. Browser choice is another option to check out. It is important that you are using the newest version of the browser for the best results. Make sure it is up to date, no matter if you are using Edge, Firefox, Mozilla, Safari, or Chrome. This update can make a world of difference.

And, of course, if all else fails, contact Cricut customer service! They are trained and knowledgeable at dealing with a host of problems. If you have a more specific problem, try browsing the solutions provided below before giving them a call, though. You just might surprise yourself with how technologically savvy you are at fixing the problem on your own!

Calibration of "Print then Cut" Is Not Working Properly

"Print then Cut" is a great feature you should consider exploring with your Cricut Explore. Basically, this function means that you print an image on your regular printer and then can put it in your Cricut Explore to cut around the edges. The first time you go to use this function, it is going to ask you to calibrate, but some people can face a frustrating situation when the machine does not read the sensor marks. Those with a Cricut Explore 1 or Cricut Air also have this function, but their machines come pre-calibrated, so this is usually not a problem for these machines.

The calibration process for the Cricut Explore includes:

1. Open Design Space and click on "Print then Cut" image, and then select "Go."
2. On your first time with this feature, the software will prompt you to print a page for calibration. This page should print on your regular printer.
3. When you have finished printing, place the page on a cutting mat and load it into your Cricut Explore. Press the "Go" button to tell the machine to cut.

4. Ideally, your machine will read the sensor marks on the calibration page and make a few test cuts and then prompt you with questions about the cuts.
5. A few more testing cuts will be made after you answer the first round of questions. After this second round of cuts, you will be asked more questions.
6. Once you finish answering all the questions, your machine will be calibrated for "Print then Cut."

For some, this process shuts down and does not complete the cut marks, meaning it cannot make it through the calibration process. There are many reasons for this, but here are a few to troubleshoot to see if one of these issues is causing it:

1. Check that your printed calibration page has all the sensor marks showing and is complete. Sometimes the file from Design Space does not get read properly by your printer and it can trim the sensor marks off. If this happens to you, go to the website for Cricut and download the calibration page from there. Print that one and make sure the sensor marks are correct. This is usually the best fix for this problem.
2. Adjust the lighting in your room. Sometimes a very brightly lit room can cause a misreading of the sensor marks. Adjust your lighting so it is softer and try again.

3. Clean off your cutting mat. A dirty mat can cause a misreading of your calibration page or it does not stay in place when cutting. Try cleaning it off and trying it again, or use a different cutting mat if you have one.
4. Check the alignment of your calibration page on your cutting mat. Make sure you placed it in the correct spot for the process. Adjust as necessary and try cutting again.

If none of these solutions fix your problem, try contacting Cricut for more assistance. There may be something else wrong with your machine or materials.

The Incorrect Cartridge Name Appears on the Cricut Screen

Follow the next steps to correct the error:

1. Sometimes in manufacturing, the cartridge stickers are placed backward on the cartridge. Take out the inserted cartridge and reinsert it backward to check if this is the problem. If this does not solve the problem, move to the next step.
2. Does this happen with all cartridges?
    a) Yes—Move to the next step.

- **b)** No—Call customer service or chat online with customer service if it still displays the wrong name after putting it in backward.
3. A hard reset may be required at this point. Follow the directions in the user manual for this. Again, if this does not fix the problem, move to the next step.
4. Update Firmware, especially if it is not up to date. If this does not fix the problem, move to the next step.
5. Call customer service or chat online with customer service if none of the above steps solved the problem.

When Images Are Added to the Queue, the Cricut Machine Freezes

Before selecting the image keys, always select the gray feature keys.

Follow the next steps to correct the error if it is still occurring:

1. Turn off the Cricut and let it rest for up to one hour. Let it rest for at least 10 minutes.
2. Double-check how the characters were entered. Try re-entering the characters in the accurate order allowing the image to show up on the screen before keying in the subsequent character.

3. "Characters won't fit" appears when the image memory is exceeded in the queue. Try removing images to see if the problem is fixed. If the problem continues, proceed to the next step.
4. If you insert another cartridge, does this error still occur?
    a) Yes—Move to the next step.
    b) No—Call customer service or chat online customer service to speak with them about the error.
5. A hard reset may be required at this point. Follow the directions in the user manual for this. Again, if this does not fix the problem, move to the next step.
6. Update Firmware, especially if it is not up to date. If this does not fix the problem, move to the next step.
7. Call customer service or chat online with customer service if none of the above steps solved the problem.

The Cricut Machine Keypad Has Glitches

There are two common keyboard errors that occur: the buttons do not respond when pressed and none of the buttons will work despite lights being lit on the keyboard. If this does not explain your problem, call customer service or chat online with customer service about the problem. If your error is one of the two most common problems, follow the steps below for whichever your problem is.

Non-Responsive Buttons When Pressed

1. Check that the machine recognizes the inserted cartridge by making sure the screen displays the cartridge's name. If this does not fix the problem, move to the next step.
2. Check that the mat is loaded into the machine properly. If this does not fix the problem, move to the next step.
3. If you insert another cartridge, does this error still occur?
    a) Yes—Move to the next step.
    b) No—Call customer service or chat online customer service to speak with them about the error.
4. A hard reset may be required at this point. Follow the directions in the user manual for this. Again, if this does not fix the problem, move to the next step.
5. Update Firmware, especially if it is not up to date. If this does not fix the problem, move to the next step.
6. Call customer service or chat online with customer service if none of the above steps solved the problem.

No Buttons Will Respond Despite Lights Coming On

1. Update Firmware, especially if it is not up to date. Lights on the left side of the keyboard, the power button, and the cut button will light up when in Firmware mode. If this does not fix the problem, move to the next step.

2. Call customer service or chat online with customer service if the above step did not solve the problem.

Unloading or Loading the Mat Makes the Cricut Machine Freeze

Follow the next steps to correct the error:

1. Turn off the Cricut and let it rest for up to one hour. Let it rest for at least 10 minutes.

2. Did you switch a cartridge while the machine was on? This is called "hot swapping" and can result in the machine freezing.

    a) Yes—Turn off your machine and switch the cartridge. If this does not solve the problem, move to the next step.

    b) No—Move to the next step.

3. If you insert another cartridge, does this error still occur?

    a) Yes—Move to the next step.

    b) No—Call customer service or chat online customer service to speak with them about the error.

4. A hard reset may be required at this point. Follow the directions in the user manual for this. Again, if this does not fix the problem, move to the next step.

5. Update Firmware, especially if it is not up to date. If this does not fix the problem, move to the next step.

6. Call customer service or chat online with customer service if none of the above steps solved the problem.

During Cutting, the Carriage Does Not Travel Along the Track

Follow the next steps to correct the error:

1. Can the carriage car move easily to the right and left while the machine is on?
    a) YES—Move to the next step.
    b) NO—Call customer service or chat online customer service to speak with them about the problem.
2. Look carefully at the belt, roller bars, and carriage car to see if any damage is evident. Take photos of any observed damage and call customer service or chat online customer service to speak with them about the problem.
    a) Belt—Is it lose or broken?
    b) Carriage car—Is it on the track? Is it on the track straight?
3. Call customer service or chat online customer service to speak with them about the problem if no damage is obvious.

When Loaded into the Cricut Machine, the Mat Becomes Crooked

Do not hold the corners or sides of the mat when loading it. Instead, hold the bottom in the center and position the mat slightly under and against the roller bar's rubber rings. This is easier when the bottom of the mat is lifted gently.

Follow the next steps to correct the error:

1. Look carefully at the roller bar to see if any damage is evident. Take photos of any observed damage and call customer service or chat online customer service to speak with them about the problem. If there is no damage noticeable, move on to the next step.
2. The correct mat size must be used for the machine. Double-check if it is correct. If this does not fix the problem, move on to the next step.
3. Before loading the mat, make sure it is aligned with guides, and the mat's edges are below the roller bar. If this does not fix the problem, move on to the next step.
4. As the roller bar begins to roll, lightly press the mat underneath with gentle pressure.
5. Call customer service or chat online with customer service if none of the above steps solved the problem.

During Cutting, the Machine Freezes

Follow the following steps to correct the error:

1. Turn off the Cricut and let it rest for up to one hour. Let it rest for at least 10 minutes.
2. If you insert another cartridge, does this error still occur?
    a) Yes—Move to the next step.
    b) No—Call customer service or chat online customer service to speak with them about the error.
3. A hard reset may be required at this point. Follow the directions in the user manual for this. Again, if this does not fix the problem, move to the next step.
4. Update Firmware, especially if it is not up to date. If this does not fix the problem, move to the next step.
5. Call customer service or chat online with customer service if none of the above steps solved the problem.

Red Banner Error Messages in Design Space

Occasionally, you will encounter an error message in Design Space that you cannot resolve with any of the tips above. When this happens, and you see one of the following messages, work through the suggestions here according to the device you are working on.

Typical error messages include:

- "Project Not Loading"
- "Custom Materials Warning"
- "Project Retrieval Error"
- "Unable to Load Pen Colors"

Other times, you will receive many errors at once. All of these warrant a different approach and perspective to your troubleshooting process.

To begin, consider closing down the software program and re-launch. This means "exit" or "quit." This is also a good time to clear your Internet's cookies and cache if you have not already done so. If this simple approach does not fix your error messages, you may want to clear your "DNS" cache. To clear this, you will need to approach it in a different way according to your operating system.

For Windows users:

1. Open your Start menu.
2. Open or choose Command Prompt, sometimes requiring you to right-click to open properly.

3. Windows 7 & 8: Enter "cmd" in the search bar and select "Command Prompt." Then select "Run as Administrator."
4. Windows 10: Right-click the Start menu and select "Command Prompt (Admin),"
5. Enter "ipconfig/flushdns."
6. The system is now going to run the process and let you know when it is done.
7. When done, type in "exit."

Now go back to Design Space and try again to see if your errors are resolved.

In general, one of the best places to find help troubleshooting a problem or error is on the Cricut website or by calling a representative. There are a host of suggestions online that you could try in addition to these, such as reconfiguring your ISP server to a Google Public DNS server, but it is best to leave those types of fixes to the IT professionals.

Conclusion

Beauty is a thing of joy forever; someone has said this. Nature itself is very beautiful. Using artificial tools and things to create something beautiful with just one natural idea is a quality of human. Manmade thing and natural thing, your surrounding is abundant with it. Creativity comes from the soul, artists are not born only sometimes artistic things come to you by practicing more and more. Translating your soul into creativity in the dimension of using vinyl craft gives you very fabulous items or products. Human always wants a variety of things around his surroundings. Creative arts fascinate them and motivate them. Getting bored by boring things is common, but creativity freshens you up.

Innovation along with technology and science gives you the finest product. The field of art and crafts is encouraged; their importance is understandable in today's world. Vinyl craft is adding another new chapter in the world of art and craft. The material used in vinyl art is very cheaper and easily available in the market. Only you need to gain a little knowledge about vinyl crafting, get a bit experience with its use and you are ready to make something very creative and useable. Use and implication of vinyl art is very wide. Rest is all about your idea your way of judging the beauty and looking perception.

If you have worked your way through the projects in this book, you are well on your way to becoming a Cricut pro. Like a recipe book, the projects, along with the ideas in this book, can be adjusted, adapted, and added to so that you can make each one uniquely yours.

With Cricut, you are going to find birthdays, special occasions, seasonal holidays, and even school projects that are a lot easier as well as more personalized. Everyone loves receiving gifts, cards, and so on, that have been designed especially for them.

You do not have to stop at just making gifts for family and friends; you can even sell your specially designed crafts at markets or online.

Happy Cricutting and keep crafty!

Printed in Great Britain
by Amazon